THE FRITZ WEEKLY READER

52 weeks of Leadership

By **Todd Douglas Fritz**

Published in the United States of America.

First Edition: 2026

ISBN 979-8-9953098-0-2

Cover Design: QLOS

Printed in the United States of America.

TABLE OF CONTENTS

OPENING NOTE

There's a moment in every leader's life when you realize you've been shaped by more than the titles you held, the missions you completed, or the people you led. You've been shaped by the moments that tested you, humbled you, broke you open, and rebuilt you.

This book wasn't written to impress anyone.
It wasn't written to teach from a pedestal.
It wasn't written to pretend I have all the answers.

It was written because leadership is human.
It's messy.
It's quiet.
It's earned.
And it's lived one moment at a time.

Every week in this book came from a place of truth — moments that shaped me, challenged me, or clarified something I didn't understand until life forced me to. Some were painful. Some were humbling. Some were simple. All of them were real.

If these pages gave you clarity, strength, or a sense of companionship on your own path, then the book did its job.

And if you're still breathing, you're not done.

Keep going.
Keep leading.
Keep becoming.

— Todd Fritz

A NOTE ON HOW TO READ THIS BOOK

This book wasn't written to be rushed.
It was written to be **walked through**.

Each chapter represents a single week — a moment, not a lesson. The intention isn't volume or velocity, but reflection. Read one week at a time. Sit with it. Let it do its work before moving on.

The book unfolds in **four seasons**, each reflecting a phase most leaders experience:

Becoming — the early days, where responsibility arrives before confidence.

Breaking / Awakening — the moments where ego collides with reality and growth begins.

Refining — the quieter work of discipline, consistency, and self-mastery.

Leading — where leadership becomes stewardship, and legacy starts to matter more than recognition.

You may recognize yourself strongly in one season.
You may find yourself moving back and forth between them.
That's normal. Leadership is not linear.

Some weeks will feel affirming.
Some will feel uncomfortable.
If something stings, pay attention — that's often where the work is.

This isn't a book to "finish."
It's a companion to return to — weekly, seasonally, honestly.

DEDICATION

For the ones who kept me alive — in body, in spirit, and in purpose.

For my partner, who held the light for me in times of darkness

For the leaders who showed me what right looks like, and for the ones who showed me what wrong looks like — both shaped me.

For every Airman, Soldier, Sailor, Marine, and Guardian who trusted me with their effort.

For the *quiet professionals* who lead without applause.

And for anyone who has ever had to rebuild themselves from the inside out.

This book is for you.

SEASON I

BECOMING

Every leader starts somewhere — usually unsure, usually unpolished, usually unaware of the weight they're stepping into. Season I is about the early moments that shape you before you even realize you're being shaped. The lessons here are foundational, raw, and often learned the hard way. This is where the journey begins.

WEEK 1

OUTSIDE THE WIRE

"The first steps that make you a leader are the ones you take on ground that might kill you — and you take them anyway." - *Todd Fritz*

There are stories from Afghanistan that sound dramatic when you tell them years later but didn't feel dramatic at the time. They just felt necessary. This is one of those.

Going outside the wire alone in Helmand Province wasn't just unusual — it bordered on suicidal. This wasn't some quiet corner of the war. This was Taliban country, the heart of the world's opium trade, and one of the most dangerous places on the planet. Even if the mines and IEDs didn't get you, the people who planted them might. We were setting up camp in their backyard, and they reminded us of that fact regularly with rockets, mortars, grenades, and small arms fire.

The terrain around our FOB wasn't just dangerous — it was littered with mines, IEDs, and unexploded ordnance of every imaginable type. Some were old Russian tank mines so rusted and unstable they had effectively become massive antipersonnel devices. The kind where, if you hit one, at least you knew it would be quick.

No one walked that ground unless they absolutely had to.

And on that day, I had to.

My team and I were on an inlieuof deployment, working with a skeleton crew in a province that didn't forgive mistakes. We had built the FOB for our Army counterparts, and because of that relationship, units from the 82nd and 101st Airborne came to us with a problem.

They needed the FOB expanded to support their AH64 and UH60 helicopter operations. The issue wasn't the construction — we could build anything. The issue was the ground. Before anything could be expanded, someone had to survey it. Someone had to walk it.

They asked if it was possible.

In REDHORSE, we don't run decisions up the chain unless we absolutely have to. If you're on site and placed in charge of the mission, you're expected to make the call. That's the culture. That's the trust. That's the burden. "Can Do, Will Do, Have Done" isn't a slogan — it's the operating system. And my first Horse unit's motto, *Semper Ducimus* — "Always Leading" — wasn't just a bumper sticker. It was the expectation.

So, I made the decision.

This should have gone to the commanding general.

But there wasn't time for ISAF and USFOR-A red tape.

This needed to be done quickly and quietly.

Consequences be damned.

"I'll do it," I told them. "But I'm not putting my people in harm's way."

Only after the decision was made did I prepare myself for what I was about to walk into. Before the mission, I went to the local bazaar and bought one of the traditional man-dress outfits the locals wore. Not because I thought it made me invisible — nothing makes an American invisible in Helmand — but because anything that reduced attention, even a little, was worth it. Underneath it, I wore a plate carrier and kept my M4 Rifle collapsed tight against my body. It wasn't comfortable, but comfort wasn't the goal. Blending in just enough to buy myself a few seconds of confusion was.

I didn't take a security element with me. I went completely solo. The only support I used was placing a couple of my men in the guard towers with the ANA. Their job wasn't to protect me out there — it was to watch the ANA on my return. If an ANA soldier raised a weapon at me, my men would see it. And if I got shot, at least I knew my guys would return the favor.

Leadership isn't complicated when you strip it down. If there's a risk, you're not willing to hand to your people, then you take it yourself. That's the job. That's the weight. That's the truth.

So, I went.

The moment I stepped outside the wire, the air changed. Helmand has a smell — a mix of moon dust, diesel, sweat, and something metallic underneath it all. It's the smell of a place that has seen too much death and hasn't forgotten any of it. The heat hit me immediately, the kind that stings your eyes and dries your throat before you even swallow. Sweat rolled down my face so fast it blurred the readings on my equipment. I had to wipe my eyes constantly just to see the numbers.

The ground was uneven, cracked, and angry. Every step felt like a negotiation. I wasn't worried about being seen — I was worried about what was under my feet. Mines don't care about uniforms, flags, or intentions. They don't care if you're building a FOB or trying to kill someone. They just wait.

I moved slowly, methodically, deliberately.

One step.
Pause.
Check the ground.

Place the rod.
Record the point.
Move again.

I shot one thousand survey points in a matter of hours. One thousand times I pushed a metal rod into soil that had been seeded with explosives for decades. One thousand times I wondered if this was the one that would end the story. You don't think about it dramatically in the moment—you think about it practically. You think about angles, distances, shadows, pressure plates, disturbed earth, and the weight of your own footsteps.

The silence wasn't really silence. It was the kind of quiet where your ears strain for anything—a click, a shift, a breath of wind that doesn't feel right. Every sound becomes a question. Every shadow becomes a possibility. Every instinct becomes a tool.

Hours passed like that.

Heat.
Sweat.
Dust.
Rod in the ground.
Move.
Repeat.

By the time I finished the last point, my hands were shaking from dehydration and adrenaline. I didn't celebrate. I didn't even feel relief. I just turned and started the long walk back toward the FOB.

That walk was its own kind of tension. You're tired, you're hot, you're mentally drained, and that's exactly when mistakes happen. I kept my pace steady, my breathing controlled, my eyes scanning everything. The towers came into view, and I knew my men were watching. Not the ground—the ANA.

I trusted my team.

I didn't trust everyone else.

When I finally stepped back inside the wire, I made it a few steps inside the compound before the world tilted. The heat, the dehydration, the hours of tension — it all hit at once. I went down hard. My team got me into a bed, and I stayed there for what seemed days, barely able to move. That's the part no one sees. That's the cost no one talks about.

But the mission was done.
The survey was complete.
The expansion could begin.
Lives would be protected.

That was the job.

And it got done.

No medals.
No speeches.
No one outside a handful of people ever knew.

But that's leadership in places like Helmand.

You don't do it for recognition.
You don't do it for glory.
You do it because someone has to — and you're not willing to hand that risk to someone you're responsible for.

Semper Ducimus.
Always Leading.

Leadership Takeaway

Leadership isn't proven in the moments when everyone is watching. It's proven in the moments when no one is.

In Helmand, the decision wasn't about courage — it was about responsibility. Leaders don't hand their people a risk they aren't willing to shoulder themselves. They don't wait for permission when the mission demands action. They don't hide behind process when lives are on the line.

Leadership is quiet.
Leadership is deliberate.
Leadership is accountable.
Leadership is always leading — especially when the ground beneath your feet might kill you.

"The first steps that make you a leader are the ones you take on ground that might kill you — and you take them anyway."

WEEK 2

LEADERS CHALLENGE ASSUMPTIONS

"Plans are suggestions. Reality is the standard." — Todd Fritz

Some leadership moments don't come with danger, adrenaline, or crisis.

Some come disguised as routine decisions — the kind everyone nods through because "that's the plan," and no one wants to slow things down.

This was one of those moments.

We were rerouting a river through the center of a military installation — a massive, complex project with tight timelines and limited real estate. The contractor needed to move a "large amount of soil," and their plan seemed simple enough: haul it to another base on the north side of the island, store it there, and bring it back when the site was ready for fill.

On paper, it looked fine.

But something about it didn't sit right.

I knew the area.
I knew the Statement of Work.

And I knew enough to know that *"large amount of soil"* was probably an understatement.

So I asked for the details.

When the numbers came back, they weren't just large — they were staggering.

7.9 million cubic feet.
300,000 cubic yards.
Enough to fill **fourteen American football fields to the goalposts**.

And the plan was to move all of it through a **single commercial gate**.

One gate.
Thirty thousand truckloads.
Two hundred fifty trucks a day.
For four straight months.

If we accepted that plan, the installation would choke.
Operations would grind to a halt.
The local community would suffer.
And the mission would pay the price.

Everyone else seemed ready to accept it.

But leadership isn't about accepting what's handed to you.
Leadership is about challenging what doesn't make sense.

So, the Japanese Engineer, my Deputy Direct, and myself sat down with the maps, the numbers, and the assumptions baked into the plan.

And we asked the question no one else had asked:

"Why does the soil have to leave the installation at all?"

That single question changed everything.

We worked with the GIS team and studied the installation map.
We looked for alternatives.

We challenged the assumption that the soil *had* to be moved off-site. And then we found it.

A recently demolished area near the project site — cleared, unused, and ready for turnover. With a few calculations and a revision to the land-use agreement, we realized we could store the soil there.

No trucking.
No gridlock.
No four-month traffic nightmare.
No operational shutdown.

Just a smarter solution.

We delayed the turnover, lifted the height restriction, and placed the soil on-site.

The result:

- Avoided **250+ dump trucks per day**
- Preserved installation operations
- Reduced burden on the local community
- Shortened project duration by **37,500 man-hours**
- Cut truck time from **1.5 hours to 15 minutes**

All because we refused to rubber-stamp a bad plan simply because it was the plan.

Leadership Takeaway

Leadership isn't about having all the answers.
It's about asking the right questions.

It's about refusing to accept assumptions at face value.
It's about seeing the second and third-order effects.
It's about stepping back far enough to see the whole field.
It's about creating space for your team — across cultures, roles, and expertise — to find a better way.

Because the truth is simple:

Leaders challenge assumptions.
Leaders think beyond the obvious.
Leaders protect the mission from the consequences no one else sees.

"Plans are suggestions. Reality is the standard."

WEEK 3

THE POWER OF SHOWING UP

"A leader's presence steadies the team. A leader's consistency strengthens it" Todd Fritz

There's a story from the **1964 Winter Olympics in Innsbruck** that almost no one talks about — not because it wasn't dramatic, but because it wasn't flashy. It didn't involve a gold medal moment or a world record. It wasn't televised triumph. It was something quieter, heavier, and far more human.

It was the story of a man who showed up when it mattered most — not to win, but to stand beside someone who couldn't stand alone.

The Forgotten Night in Innsbruck

During the two-man bobsled competition, the British team suffered a catastrophic crash. Their brakeman, Tony Nash, survived with injuries. But his teammate — Robin Dixon — was shaken, bruised, and emotionally rattled. The crash had been violent enough that the sled splintered, and the team's Olympic hopes were effectively over.

But the story isn't about the crash.

It's about what happened afterward.

That night, long after the crowds left and the cameras shut off, the Italian bobsledder **Eugenio Monti** — already a legend in the sport — walked quietly into the British quarters. He wasn't there for strategy. He wasn't there for publicity. He wasn't even there as a competitor.

He was there because he knew what it felt like to be broken, to be shaken, to be staring at the ground wondering if you could get back up.

Monti didn't give a speech.
He didn't offer advice.
He didn't talk about courage or resilience.

He just sat with them.

He checked on their injuries.
He helped them repair what equipment they could salvage.
He stayed until the room steadied.
He showed up — not as a rival, but as a human being.

The next morning, the British team returned to the track. They didn't win a medal. They didn't set a record. But they finished — bruised, battered, and carried forward by the quiet presence of someone who didn't owe them anything.

Monti would later win the Pierre de Coubertin Medal — the highest honor for sportsmanship — but that night in the British quarters wasn't about awards.

It was about presence.

It was about leadership.

It was about showing up when someone else needed steadiness more than you needed sleep.

The Weight of Showing Up

Leadership books love the big moments — the speeches, the breakthroughs, the dramatic turning points. But most leadership doesn't happen in the spotlight. It happens in the quiet rooms after the crash. It happens in the moments when someone is shaken, uncertain, or carrying more than they can say out loud.

Showing up isn't glamorous.
It isn't loud.
It isn't heroic.

It's weight.

It's responsibility.

It's the steadying force that tells people:

"You're not alone in this. I'm here. We'll face it together."

Monti didn't fix the British sled.
He didn't erase the crash.
He didn't change the outcome.

But he changed the moment.

And sometimes, that's the difference between someone giving up and someone getting back in the sled.

What Presence Communicates

When a leader shows up — physically, emotionally, consistently — it communicates things no speech ever could:

- **Stability** — "The ground isn't shifting beneath you."
- **Respect** — "Your struggle matters enough for me to be here."
- **Commitment** — "I'm not leaving you to carry this alone."
- **Trust** — "You're worth my time, even when there's nothing to gain."

- **Humanity** — “This isn’t about winning. This is about us.”

Presence is leadership in its most human form.

When You Don’t Show Up

Absence creates stories.
Presence creates stability.

When leaders disappear during hard moments, people don’t assume they’re busy — they assume they don’t care. And once that belief takes root, it’s almost impossible to uproot.

Showing up doesn’t solve everything.
But not showing up solves nothing.

Leadership Takeaway

Leadership isn’t about being impressive.
It’s about being present.

It’s about the quiet, steady weight of showing up — not to fix everything, but to stand beside the people who need you most.

Because the truth is simple:

A leader’s presence steadies the team.
A leader’s consistency strengthens it.

WEEK 4

THE LEADER WHO SETS THE EXAMPLE

"Teams don't rise to your speeches. They rise to your example."
— Todd Fritz

The Weight No One Sees

When you become a leader, you don't just gain authority. You lose anonymity.

Every move you make becomes a signal.
Every habit becomes a standard.
Every inconsistency becomes an excuse.
Every discipline becomes a culture.

People aren't watching you to judge you.
They're watching you to understand *what normal looks like.*

That's the part most leadership books skip.
But every senior enlisted leader knows it by heart.

The Tools You Hope You Never Have to Use

In REDHORSE, "eyes on the leader" isn't about catching mistakes — it's about reading the temperature of the entire unit. And sometimes, the culture needs a little... calibration.

Not punishment.
Not humiliation.
Just a reminder that standards matter.

I carried a pink hard hat covered in My Little Pony stickers and sequins.
Not because I wanted to embarrass anyone.
But because even though they are at the tip of the spear, calling a REDHORSE Combat Engineer a "Pink Pony" — especially if you aren't REDHORSE — is a fast way to get some very unwelcomed attention.

So the hard hat wasn't a joke.
It was a message.

If you were sloppy, careless, or cutting corners, you knew Chief Fritz might hand you that hard hat to wear for the day.

But here's the thing:

No one ever had to wear it.
They just had to know it existed.

The best weapon is the one you never have to use.

Same with the 30pound chain.

If someone bypassed the chain of command, they wore the chain for a day.
If it kept happening, their supervisor wore it — because now *they* were the one failing.

Not as punishment.
As clarity.

Colin Powell said it best:
"When your people stop bringing you problems, you've stopped leading them."

The chain wasn't about weight.
It was about responsibility.

And just like the hard hat, no one ever had to wear it.

Because the example was enough.

The Mirror Effect

Leadership is a mirror.

Whatever you do, your team will reflect.

- If you're calm under pressure, they steady themselves.
- If you cut corners, they cut deeper.
- If you show up late, they show up later.
- If you gossip, they divide.
- If you hustle, they hustle harder.

You don't get to opt out of this.
You don't get to say, "Do as I say, not as I do."
That's not leadership.
That's hypocrisy.

And people can smell it a mile away.

The Identity Shift No One Warns You About

The deeper truth behind "setting the example" isn't about rules or compliance.

It's about identity.

The moment you become a leader:

- Your habits become culture.

- Your flaws become permission slips.
- Your discipline becomes the standard.
- Your inconsistency becomes the excuse.
- Your behavior becomes the blueprint for everyone else's.

This is the part no one tells you about.

Leadership doesn't just change your responsibilities.
It changes what your actions *mean*.

The Power of Alignment

When your actions match your words, something powerful happens:

- Trust increases
- Clarity sharpens
- Culture strengthens
- Accountability becomes shared
- Standards become self-enforced

You don't have to micromanage.
You don't have to repeat yourself.
You don't have to chase compliance.

Because your team isn't following rules.
They're following *you*.

The Cost of Inconsistency

But when your actions and words don't align, the cost is steep:

- Morale drops
- Trust erodes
- Cynicism grows
- Performance suffers

People don't rebel against rules.
They rebel against hypocrisy.

The Quiet Power of Example

Setting the example doesn't mean being perfect.
It means being intentional.

It means asking yourself:

- What do I want this team to value?
- What do I want this team to believe?
- What do I want this team to become?

Then living that out — visibly, consistently, and without exception.

If you want a team that's disciplined, be disciplined.
If you want a team that communicates, communicate.
If you want a team that owns mistakes, own yours first.
If you want a team that cares, show them what care looks like.

Because the truth is, your team is always learning from you.

The only question is what you're teaching them.

Leadership Takeaway

This week isn't about control.
It's about credibility.

And the deeper truth is this:

Setting the example isn't about being watched.
It's about being worth watching.

WEEK 5

THE LEADER WHO BRINGS CLARITY

"A leader's first responsibility is clarity. Everything else depends on it."
— Todd Fritz

The Most Dangerous Leader in Any Organization

The most dangerous leader isn't the one who lacks confidence. It's the one who has confidence **without clarity**.

Confidence without clarity looks like strength, but it behaves like turbulence. It creates motion without direction, noise without meaning, and activity without progress. And in any high-stakes environment — construction, operations, business, emergency response, or any place where people rely on each other — that kind of leadership isn't just inefficient.

It's dangerous.

Because people will follow a confident leader... even when that leader is confidently wrong.

Clarity as a Force Multiplier

Clarity is not a soft skill. Clarity is a force multiplier.

It sharpens decision-making.
It accelerates execution.
It reduces friction.
It aligns effort.
It prevents rework, confusion, and drift.

A clear leader can take an average team and make them exceptional. An unclear leader can take an exceptional team and make them average.

Clarity multiplies everything it touches — discipline, trust, tempo, and performance.

Clarity as a Moral Responsibility

When you lead people, you owe them clarity.

Not because it's efficient.
Because it's ethical.

People can't follow what they don't understand.
They can't execute what hasn't been defined.
They can't prioritize what hasn't been explained.

Unclear leaders force their teams to guess.
And guessing is not a leadership strategy — it's a liability.

Clarity protects people from unnecessary risk, wasted effort, and preventable failure.

Clarity as the Antidote to False Confidence

There's a particular kind of leader who is loud, certain, and wrong. They speak with authority but without understanding. They lead with position instead of competence. They confuse decisiveness with wisdom.

Every industry has them.

The executive who walks in with a plan built on assumptions instead of facts.
The manager who mistakes volume for vision.
The leader who believes confidence alone will carry the day.

It won't.

Confidence without clarity doesn't inspire. It endangers.

And when that kind of leader is in charge, the failures aren't small. They're systemic.

You've seen it:
High confidence.
Low clarity.
No depth.
No understanding of the operational reality.
And the fallout is predictable — wasted resources, fractured teams, lost trust, and outcomes that fail in ways that could have been prevented.

False confidence is not a leadership trait. It's a warning sign.

Clarity as the Foundation of Trust

People don't need their leader to be perfect. They need their leader to be clear.

Clarity builds trust because it removes ambiguity. It tells people:

- What matters
- What doesn't
- Where we're going
- Why it matters
- What success looks like
- What their role is in achieving it

When people understand the mission, they commit to it.
When they understand the standard, they rise to it.
When they understand the "why," they fight for it.

Clarity is the foundation of trust — and trust is the foundation of every high-performing team.

Turning Intent Into Vision

In any organization, clarity begins with intent — the leader's desired outcome, purpose, and priorities.

But intent is not execution.
Intent is not a plan.
Intent is not a vision.

That translation is the responsibility of the senior leaders closest to the work.

Their job isn't to repeat the intent.
Their job is to **interpret** it.

To take broad direction and turn it into:

- Actionable steps
- Realistic timelines

- Defined priorities
- A vision the team can actually execute

This is where clarity becomes leadership. It's the bridge between strategy and reality, between what the organization wants and what the team needs.

When that translation is done well, the mission moves.
When it's done poorly — or not at all — the mission stalls.

Clarity is the difference.

The Cost of Unclear Leadership

Unclear leadership doesn't just slow teams down. It breaks them.

It creates:

- Confusion
- Frustration
- Rework
- Misalignment
- Safety risks
- Talent loss
- Cynicism
- Erosion of trust

People don't leave organizations. They leave unclear leaders.

And the talent that walks out the door because they were confused, ignored, or misled?
You don't replace that. You rebuild around the hole they leave behind.

The Quiet Power of Clear Leadership

Clear leaders don't need to shout. They don't need to posture. They don't need to prove themselves.

They define the mission.
They define the standard.
They define the path.
They define the "why."

And then they get out of the way and let their people execute.

Clarity creates confidence.
Confidence creates momentum.
Momentum creates results.

This is leadership at its highest level — not loud, not flashy, not dramatic.

Just clear.

Leadership Takeaway

Clarity is not optional. It is the first responsibility of leadership.

Because when leaders are unclear, teams hesitate.
When leaders are clear, teams move.

Everything a leader hopes to build — trust, momentum, confidence, culture, results — begins with clarity.

When you bring clarity, everything else has a place to stand.

WEEK 6

THE LEADER WHO LISTENS FIRST

"If you want the truth, be quiet long enough for people to trust you with it."
— Todd Fritz

The Kind of Silence That Changes a Room

There's a kind of silence that makes people nervous. And there's a kind of silence that makes people feel safe. Leaders create one or the other.

During a tense stretch in a joint environment — high tempo, strong personalities, constant pressure — I walked into a team that felt unheard. Not ignored. *Unheard*. There's a difference.

I didn't start with a speech. I didn't start with a plan.

I walked to the whiteboard, uncapped the marker, and wrote one word:

"WHY?"

Not "Why aren't you speaking up?"
Not "Why is morale low?"
Not "Why are things broken?"

This **WHY** was bigger than that. It meant:

- Why are *you* here?
- Why are *we* here?
- Why are we doing it this way?
- Why hasn't this been fixed?
- Why haven't we automated this?
- Why is this still acceptable?
- Why is the truth not surfacing?

It was a question about purpose, process, culture, and accountability — all at once.

And then I stopped talking.

Because the leader who speaks last hears the most.

The Power of the Pause

At first, the silence was awkward. People weren't used to being asked what they thought — and they definitely weren't used to being given space to answer.

But I waited. I let the silence stretch. I let the discomfort settle.

And then it happened.

One by one, they started to talk.

Not about tasks.
Not about checklists.
Not about the daily grind.

They talked about the culture.
The fear.
The burnout.
The things they'd been carrying but hadn't felt safe enough to say.

And once it started, it didn't stop.

Because here's the truth:
People want to be heard more than they want to be fixed — and the best advice you'll ever get often shows up in the exit interview, when it's too late to act on it.

That's the cost of leaders who don't listen:
They lose their best people *and* their best information.

Listening Is Not Passive

Listening isn't sitting quietly. Listening is work.

It's reading the room.
It's watching body language.
It's **noticing what isn't said**.
It's noticing **who** isn't saying it.
It's resisting the urge to jump in with solutions.
It's letting people finish their sentences — and their thoughts.

Most leaders listen to respond.
Great leaders listen to understand.
The best leaders listen to *learn*.

What Listening Creates

When people feel heard, they give you:

- Honesty
- Insight
- Trust
- Commitment
- Early warnings
- Better solutions

Listening is one of the most powerful tools a leader has — and one of the least used. Because listening requires humility. And humility is rare.

The Cost of Not Listening

When leaders don't listen, teams don't stay silent.

They shut down.
They stop sharing ideas.
They stop raising concerns.
They stop telling the truth.

And once that happens, the mission suffers long before anyone realizes why.

Silence isn't the absence of noise.
It's the absence of trust.

And the talent that leaves because they weren't heard?
You don't replace that. You rebuild around the hole they leave behind.

Asking "Why?" Is Only the Beginning

Asking **WHY** is not the finish line. It's the starting point.

Because once a leader asks Why, they inherit a responsibility:

- To understand the answer
- To act on the answer
- To communicate what will be done
- To show people they were heard
- To close the loop

If a leader asks Why, gets the truth, and does nothing with it, that is worse than never asking at all. It breaks trust twice — once for the silence, and again for the inaction.

And the deeper truth is this:

Why leads to What.
What leads to Who.

Who leads to When.
And eventually, every real leader must get to HOW.

The 5 W's and the H aren't just a framework. They're a road-map for leaders who want to turn listening into progress.

The Quiet Strength of Listening First

Listening first doesn't make a leader passive. It makes them precise.

It gives them the full picture before they act.
It gives them the truth before they decide.
It gives them the trust they need to lead.

Speaking last isn't weakness. It's discipline.
It's the leader saying, "Your voice matters before mine."

And that changes everything.

Leadership Takeaway

This week isn't about communication. It's about connection.

Because the truth is simple:

If you want the truth, create space for it to be spoken — and be the last one in the room to speak.

WEEK 7

THE LEADER WHO MAKES ACCOUNTABILITY SAFE

"Accountability isn't about blame. It's about truth — and truth only shows up where it feels safe." — Todd Fritz

The Moment Accountability Becomes Culture

Every team has problems.
Every team makes mistakes.
Every team misses something.

The difference between high-performing teams and struggling ones isn't whether mistakes happen — it's **what happens next**.

In weak cultures, mistakes get buried.
In fearful cultures, mistakes get hidden.
In toxic cultures, mistakes get weaponized.

But in strong cultures — the kind leaders build with intention — mistakes become information. They become learning. They become alignment. They become the moment the team gets better.

And that only happens when accountability is safe.

Accountability Begins With Safety, Not Blame

Most people don't fear accountability.
They fear the consequences of honesty.

They fear:

- Being embarrassed
- Being singled out
- Being punished
- Being labeled
- Being ignored
- Being judged

So they stay quiet.
They protect themselves.
They protect their reputation.
They protect their job.

And the truth stays buried under silence.

A leader's job is to make accountability safe enough that the truth can surface before the damage does.

The Leader Sets the Tone

People watch the leader's reaction long before they share the truth.

If the leader reacts with anger, people hide.
If the leader reacts with blame, people deflect.
If the leader reacts with ego, people shut down.

But when a leader reacts with curiosity — not judgment — everything changes.

Curiosity sounds like:

- "Walk me through what happened."
- "Help me understand the decision."
- "What did we miss?"

- "What do you need next time?"
- "What would have prevented this?"

Curiosity turns mistakes into data.
Judgment turns mistakes into fear.

Accountability Is a System, Not a Moment

Accountability isn't a onetime event.
It's a structure leaders build.

Strong accountability systems include:

- **Clear expectations** — people can't be accountable for what they don't understand
- **Transparent priorities** — clarity reduces confusion
- **Psychological safety** — people speak up when they feel protected
- **Consistent follow-through** — leaders do what they say
- **Shared ownership** — the team succeeds or fails together

When these elements are in place, accountability becomes normal — not dramatic.

The Leader's Role: Make the Truth Easy to Tell

People will tell the truth when:

- They trust the leader
- They trust the process
- They trust they won't be punished for honesty
- They trust the leader will act on what they share

This is where Week 6 and Week 7 connect.

Listening creates safety.
Safety creates honesty.
Honesty creates accountability.
Accountability creates improvement.

This is the chain of leadership.

Break any link, and the whole system collapses.

The Cost of Unsafe Accountability

When accountability is unsafe, leaders don't just lose information — they lose people.

They lose:

- Initiative
- Creativity
- Candor
- Early warnings
- Engagement
- Trust
- Talent

People don't leave because of mistakes.
They leave because of the environment around them.

And the talent that walks out the door because accountability wasn't safe?
You don't replace that.
You rebuild around the hole they leave behind.

The Quiet Strength of a Leader Who Makes Accountability Safe

Leaders who make accountability safe aren't soft.
They're strong in the ways that matter.

They don't avoid hard conversations.
They don't ignore problems.
They don't pretend everything is fine.

They create a space where the truth can be spoken without fear — and once the truth is on the table, they guide the team toward solutions.

This is leadership at its highest level:
Not blame.
Not ego.
Not punishment.

Just truth, safety, and progress.

Leadership Takeaway

Accountability isn't about catching people doing something wrong. It's about creating a culture where people feel safe enough to tell the truth before the consequences get worse.

Because the truth is simple:

When leaders make accountability safe, teams stop hiding problems — and start solving them.

WEEK 8

THE LEADER WHO BUILDS BELIEF

"Performance is the outcome. Belief is the engine." — Todd Fritz

The Difference Between a Good Team and a Great One

Every team has talent. Every team has goals. Every team has pressure.

But not every team has belief.

Belief is the quiet force that turns individuals into a unit. It's what keeps people steady when the stakes rise. It's what makes a team push one more inch, one more rep, one more late night — not because they're told to, but because they *believe* in what they're doing.

And belief doesn't appear on its own.
Leaders build it.

A Lesson From a High-Performance World

In Formula One, the margins are razor thin. A tenth of a second can separate a champion from the middle of the pack. Pressure is constant. Scrutiny is relentless. The world is watching.

And yet, the teams that dominate aren't the ones with the fastest car. They're the ones with the strongest culture.

That's what makes Christian Horner's leadership so instructive.

Across 21 seasons, he led Red Bull to:

- **6 Constructors' Championships** (2010–2013, 2022–2023)
- **8 Drivers' Championships** (4 with Vettel, 4 with Verstappen)
- **124 Grand Prix victories**
- **107 pole positions**
- **287 podiums**
- **Over 8,000 championship points**
- **405 consecutive race starts as team principal**
- **The second-most wins of any team principal in F1 history**

These aren't racing statistics.
They're leadership statistics.

They represent two decades of building belief inside one of the most pressure-filled environments on earth.

Belief Is Built in the Hard Moments

Anyone can lead when things are going well.
Belief is built when they aren't.

Belief is built when:

- The team is tired
- The pressure is high
- The outcome is uncertain
- The critics are loud
- The path forward isn't obvious

This is where leaders earn their influence.

Not by giving speeches.
Not by demanding more.
Not by pretending everything is fine.

But by doing three things exceptionally well:

1. **Stabilizing the environment** — removing chaos so people can focus
2. **Reinforcing purpose** — reminding the team why the work matters
3. **Protecting the culture** — shielding the team from noise, politics, and fear

Belief grows when people feel safe, valued, and aligned.

The Leader as the Emotional Center of Gravity

In high-pressure environments, the leader becomes the emotional thermostat.

If the leader panics, the team fractures.
If the leader blames, the team hides.
If the leader wavers, the team hesitates.

But when the leader stays steady — calm, clear, consistent — the team finds its footing.

This was the defining feature of Horner's leadership.
He didn't just manage the team.
He *centered* it.

He absorbed pressure so others didn't have to.
He kept the mission simple when everything around them was complicated.
He made the team feel protected, not exposed.

That's what great leaders do.
They become the place where the team finds stability.

Belief Turns Talent Into Performance

Talent is potential.
Belief is activation.

When people believe in:

- The mission
- The leader
- The culture
- The team
- Themselves

They perform differently.

They take ownership.
They take risks.
They innovate.
They communicate.
They push through adversity.
They stay when others would quit.

Belief is the multiplier that turns a good team into a great one.

The Cost of a Leader Who Doesn't Build Belief

When leaders fail to build belief, teams don't collapse overnight.
They erode quietly.

You see:

- More hesitation
- More second-guessing
- More turnover
- More politics
- More fear
- Less initiative
- Less trust
- Less honesty

People stop giving their best when they stop believing their best matters.

And once belief is gone, performance follows.

The Quiet Strength of a Leader Who Builds Belief

Leaders who build belief aren't loud.
They aren't dramatic.
They aren't performative.

They are:

- Consistent
- Clear
- Steady
- Protective
- Purpose-driven
- Culture-focused

They don't just lead the work.
They lead the *why* behind the work.

They don't just manage performance.
They create the conditions where performance becomes inevitable.

They don't just build teams.
They build belief.

Leadership Takeaway

Belief is not a feeling.
It's a structure leaders build through clarity, consistency, and connection.

Because the truth is simple:

Performance is the outcome. Belief is the engine.

WEEK 9

THE LEADER WHO HAS HARD CONVERSATIONS

"Avoiding a hard conversation doesn't protect the relationship. It erodes it in silence." — *Todd Fritz*

The Conversation That Almost Changed the World

In October 1962, the world stood closer to nuclear war than at any other moment in history. The Cuban Missile Crisis wasn't just a geopolitical standoff — it was a masterclass in how leaders handle the hardest conversations imaginable.

Two superpowers.
Armed forces on alert.
Missiles in place.
The world watching.

And yet, the crisis didn't end in force.
It ended in a **conversation** — one that required clarity, courage, emotional control, and the discipline to stay in dialogue when everything in the environment pushed toward escalation.

This is the essence of a hard conversation:
high stakes, strong emotions, and opposing views.

Leaders face these moments every day — not with missiles, but with people.

Why Hard Conversations Matter

Hard conversations are where:

- trust is built
- expectations are clarified
- accountability is reinforced
- relationships are strengthened
- performance is corrected
- culture is protected

Avoiding them doesn't preserve harmony.
It preserves dysfunction.

Silence is not kindness.
Silence is avoidance dressed as peace.

Lessons From the Cuban Missile Crisis

The crisis revealed several leadership behaviors that apply directly to difficult conversations inside any organization.

1. Begin with purpose, not emotion

President Kennedy's team aligned around a single goal:
remove the threat without triggering war.

Leaders who start with purpose stay grounded.
Leaders who start with emotion escalate.

2. Create a space where honesty is possible

Back-channel communication allowed both sides to speak without posturing.

People tell the truth when they feel safe — not when they feel cornered.

Safety isn't softness.
Safety is strategy.

3. Separate what you know from what you fear

Kennedy's advisors distinguished **facts** (missiles in Cuba) from **assumptions** (intent to strike).

Leaders who react to assumptions create conflict.
Leaders who react to facts create solutions.

4. Stay in the conversation, even when it's uncomfortable

The crisis was resolved because both sides kept talking — even when the messages were tense, unclear, or contradictory.

Dialogue is the only path to resolution.
Silence and aggression are the two paths to failure.

5. Make the path forward safe for everyone involved

The final agreement allowed both sides to move forward without humiliation.

People move when they feel respected.
People resist when they feel threatened.

Hard Conversations Inside Organizations

Leaders face their own versions of high-stakes conversations:

- performance issues
- broken trust
- misalignment

- disrespect
- unmet expectations
- cultural violations
- accountability gaps

The stakes aren't global, but they're personal — and personal stakes feel just as heavy.

The principles remain the same:

- Start with purpose
- Create safety
- Stick to facts
- Stay in dialogue
- Move toward action

Hard conversations aren't about winning.
They're about **truth, alignment, and progress**.

The Cost of Avoiding Hard Conversations

Avoidance has a price.

You see:

- resentment
- confusion
- declining performance
- fractured relationships
- cultural drift
- loss of trust
- loss of talent

People don't leave because of the conversation you had.
They leave because of the one you avoided.

The Quiet Strength of Leaders Who Lean In

Leaders who have hard conversations aren't confrontational.
They're courageous.

They don't raise their voice.
They raise the standard.

They don't attack the person.
They address the behavior.

They don't avoid discomfort.
They navigate it.

They don't let silence do the talking.
They speak with clarity, respect, and purpose.

This is leadership at its most human — the willingness to step into discomfort for the sake of the relationship, the mission, and the culture.

Leadership Takeaway

Hard conversations aren't a sign of conflict.
They're a sign of commitment.

Because the truth is simple:

When leaders avoid hard conversations, problems grow.
When leaders have them, people do.

WEEK 10

THE LEADER WHO STAYS HUMBLE

"Humility isn't self-doubt. It's the discipline of putting purpose before ego." — Todd Fritz

The Strength to Lead Without Needing the Spotlight

Humility is one of the most misunderstood leadership traits. People mistake it for softness, modesty, or a lack of confidence. But humility is none of those things.

Humility is **discipline**.
Humility is **clarity**.
Humility is **strength under control**.

It's the ability to stay grounded when praised, steady when criticized, and focused when others get distracted by ego.

And history gives us one of the clearest examples of humility used as a strategic advantage: Abraham Lincoln's decision to build a cabinet out of the very men who ran against him.

A Lesson From a Leader Who Chose Humility Over Ego

When Lincoln won the presidency in 1860, he did something almost unthinkable: he appointed his fiercest political rivals to the most powerful positions in his administration.

These were men who:

- publicly opposed him
- underestimated him
- criticized him
- believed they were more qualified
- expected him to fail

And Lincoln brought them in anyway.

Not because he needed validation.
Not because he lacked confidence.
But because he understood something most leaders never learn:

You don't build strong teams by surrounding yourself with people who agree with you.
You build strong teams by surrounding yourself with people who challenge you.

That decision required humility — the kind that prioritizes mission over ego.

What Humility Looks Like in Leadership

Humility isn't a personality trait. It's a set of behaviors leaders choose on purpose.

1. Humility listens before it decides

Humble leaders don't assume they have the best idea in the room. They assume someone else might — and they want to hear it.

2. Humility invites challenge, not compliance

Lincoln didn't want a cabinet that echoed him.
He wanted a cabinet that sharpened him.

Humble leaders don't fear disagreement.
They fear silence.

3. Humility separates confidence from arrogance

Confidence says, "I can do this."
Arrogance says, "Only I can do this."
Humility says, "We can do this better together."

4. Humility protects the mission from ego

Ego narrows vision.
Humility widens it.

Ego demands credit.
Humility demands results.

Ego divides teams.
Humility unites them.

5. Humility keeps leaders connected to reality

The higher a leader rises, the fewer people tell them the truth.
Humility keeps the door open.

Why Humility Is a Strategic Advantage

Humility isn't about being liked.
It's about being effective.

Teams follow humble leaders because:

- they feel respected
- they feel heard
- they feel valued

- they feel safe to contribute
- they feel trusted
- they feel ownership

Humility creates an environment where people bring their best ideas forward — not because they're told to, but because they know their voice matters.

And when people feel that, performance follows.

The Cost of a Leader Without Humility

When humility is absent, ego fills the space.

You see:

- defensiveness
- blame
- insecurity
- poor decisions
- hidden problems
- talent leaving
- culture eroding

Ego makes leaders fragile.
Humility makes leaders durable.

The Quiet Strength of a Humble Leader

Humble leaders don't need the spotlight.
They don't need the credit.
They don't need to be the smartest person in the room.

They need the mission to succeed.
They need the team to thrive.
They need the truth more than they need their pride.

Humility isn't weakness.
It's wisdom.

It's the leader saying, "I don't have all the answers — but together, we will find them."

Leadership Takeaway

Humility isn't about lowering yourself.
It's about elevating the mission above your ego.

Because the truth is simple:

When leaders stay humble, teams stay honest — and honest teams win.

WEEK 11

THE STANDARD YOU HOLD WHEN NO ONE IS WATCHING

"Integrity is the standard you protect when the world expects you to compromise." — Todd Fritz

The Marine Who Refused to Look Away

Major General Smedley Darlington Butler — "Old Gimlet Eye" — was one of the most decorated Marines in American history. Two Medals of Honor. A career that spanned interventions, wars, and political storms. A leader trusted by enlisted Marines and feared by corrupt politicians.

But what makes Butler a leadership lesson isn't his combat record. It's his **integrity** — the kind that shows up when:

- no one is watching
- everyone is watching
- and the stakes are personal

Butler didn't just hold the standard.
He *protected* it — even when it cost him.

The Bonus Army: Integrity Toward People

In 1932, tens of thousands of World War I veterans marched on Washington demanding the bonuses they were promised. They were hungry, unemployed, and dismissed as troublemakers.

No one ordered Butler to go.
No one expected him to.
No one would have blamed him if he stayed home.

He went anyway.

He walked into the camps, stood on makeshift platforms, and spoke to the veterans with dignity and respect. He told them:

"You are the finest soldiers I have ever seen."

He didn't bring authority.
He brought humanity.

He didn't bring orders.
He brought truth.

He didn't bring judgment.
He brought integrity — the kind that sees people, not problems.

The Business Plot: Integrity Toward the Constitution

A year later, a group of wealthy businessmen approached Butler with a plan:
lead a coup against President Franklin Roosevelt and install a controlled "figurehead" government.

They assumed he'd say yes because:

- he was respected
- he was popular
- he was trusted by the troops
- he was a Marine
- he was a patriot

They misjudged him.

Butler listened, gathered evidence, and then did the one thing they never expected:

He exposed the plot publicly.

He testified before Congress, knowing it would make him enemies.
He chose the Constitution over personal gain.
He chose the country over influence.
He chose integrity over opportunity.

That's the standard you hold when no one is watching — and when everyone is.

War Is a Racket: Integrity Toward Truth

In his final years, Butler could have retired quietly.
He could have protected his reputation.
He could have enjoyed the comfort he earned.

Instead, he told the truth about the political and economic forces behind war — a truth that was uncomfortable, unpopular, and ahead of its time.

He said:

"War is a racket."

Not to shock.
Not to provoke.
But because he believed leaders owed their people honesty — even when honesty was inconvenient.

That's integrity.

What Butler Teaches Us About Integrity

Integrity isn't about being perfect.
It's about being **aligned** — with your values, your mission, and your people.

Butler's life shows three forms of integrity leaders must master:

1. Integrity toward people

Treating others with dignity when the world treats them as expendable.

2. Integrity toward principles

Protecting the mission, the institution, and the truth — even when it costs you.

3. Integrity toward yourself

Refusing to compromise your values for approval, advancement, or comfort.

Integrity is not a speech.
It's a pattern.

Why Integrity Matters in Leadership

Integrity is the quiet force that makes every other leadership behavior possible.

Without integrity:

- clarity becomes manipulation
- listening becomes performance
- accountability becomes punishment
- belief becomes blind loyalty
- humility becomes a tactic
- hard conversations become control

Integrity is the anchor that keeps leadership from drifting into ego, politics, or convenience.

It's the thing that makes people trust you — not because you say the right things, but because you *are* the right thing when it counts.

Integrity Under Pressure

Integrity is easy when:

- the stakes are low
- the decision is popular
- the consequences are small

Integrity becomes leadership when:

- no one will know
- no one will see
- no one will check
- no one will praise you
- no one will blame you

Butler had every opportunity to choose the easy path.
He chose the right one instead.

That's integrity with consequences.

The Quiet Strength of a Leader Who Holds the Standard

Leaders with integrity don't need to announce it.
They don't need to defend it.
They don't need to perform it.

People feel it.

Integrity creates:

- stability
- predictability
- safety
- respect
- loyalty

Integrity compounds.
Every decision adds to it or subtracts from it.

And when a leader consistently chooses integrity — especially when the world expects compromise — the team becomes stronger than any crisis, environment, or circumstance.

Leadership Takeaway

Integrity is not about being perfect.
It's about being **consistent**, **honest**, and **aligned** — especially when the easy path is available.

Because the truth is simple:

The standard you hold when no one is watching becomes the culture your people live when everyone is.

WEEK 12

THE LEADER WHO PROTECTS WHAT MATTERS

"A leader's time is a message. What you protect becomes what your people value." — Todd Fritz

The General Who Refused to Be Ruled by Urgency

In 1944, Dwight D. Eisenhower commanded the largest military operation in human history. Millions of troops. Thousands of ships. A global coalition. Every decision carried consequences measured in lives.

And yet, Eisenhower was known for something surprising:
he refused to let urgency dictate his leadership.

He understood a truth most leaders never learn:

Urgency is loud.
Importance is quiet.
And if you don't protect the quiet, the loud will consume everything.

Eisenhower didn't drown in tasks.
He didn't chase fires.
He didn't let the pace of the world set the pace of his mind.

He protected what mattered — and because he did, he could see what others missed.

Why Leaders Lose Control of Their Time

Leaders don't get overwhelmed because they're weak.
They get overwhelmed because they're responsible.

People bring them problems.
Systems bring them noise.
Organizations bring them urgency.
And the world brings them distraction.

The danger isn't the workload.
The danger is **losing the ability to choose**.

When leaders stop choosing, they stop leading.

What Eisenhower Teaches Us About Protecting What Matters

Eisenhower didn't invent the idea of prioritization — he lived it. His leadership revealed three disciplines that modern leaders still struggle with.

1. He separated noise from necessity

Eisenhower distinguished between what was **urgent** and what was **important** — not as a productivity trick, but as a leadership discipline.

Urgent things demand attention.
Important things deserve attention.

Leaders who confuse the two become reactive.
Leaders who separate them become strategic.

2. He protected time for thinking

Even during the war, Eisenhower carved out quiet time to think, reflect, and plan. Not because he had extra time — but because he didn't.

Leaders who don't think become operators.
Leaders who think become commanders.

3. He delegated authority, not tasks

Eisenhower trusted his commanders. He gave them intent, not micromanagement. He protected his attention by empowering theirs.

Delegation isn't about reducing workload.
It's about increasing clarity.

The Leadership Cost of Not Protecting What Matters

When leaders fail to protect their time, attention, and energy, the consequences are predictable:

- priorities blur
- standards slip
- decisions degrade
- morale drops
- creativity dies
- culture drifts
- burnout spreads

People don't follow exhausted leaders.
They follow present ones.

What Protecting What Matters Looks Like in Practice

This isn't about calendars or apps.
It's about **leadership posture**.

Leaders protect what matters when they:

- say no to the wrong things
- say yes to the right things
- create space for thinking
- refuse to be ruled by urgency
- delegate with clarity
- focus on outcomes, not activity
- guard their attention like a strategic asset

A leader's time is not a schedule.
It's a signal.

It tells the team what matters.
It tells the culture what to value.
It tells the mission what to expect.

The Quiet Strength of Leaders Who Protect Their Priorities

Leaders who protect what matters aren't rigid.
They're intentional.

They don't chase everything.
They choose the right things.

They don't react to noise.
They respond to purpose.

They don't drown in urgency.
They rise above it.

This is the discipline that separates leaders who survive from leaders who shape the future.

Leadership Takeaway

Leadership isn't about doing more.
It's about doing what matters — and protecting it fiercely.

Because the truth is simple:

When leaders protect what matters, teams learn what matters — and they rise to meet it.

WEEK 13

THE LEADER WHO EARNS TRUST

"Trust is built in the small moments long before it's needed in the big ones." — Todd Fritz

The Airman the Army Trusted With Their Lives

On April 11, 1966, an Army infantry unit walked into an ambush near Cam My, Vietnam. They were outnumbered, out-gunned, and taking heavy casualties. Medevac helicopters tried to reach them, but the landing zone was too hot.

Then a pararescueman — **Airman First Class William H. "Pits" Pitsenbarger** — volunteered to be lowered through enemy fire to help the wounded.

He wasn't ordered.
He wasn't expected to.
He wasn't supposed to.

He went because the soldiers on the ground needed someone they could trust.

And trust isn't built in the moment you're lowered into a firefight. It's built in the hundreds of moments before — in the way you train, the way you prepare, the way you carry yourself, and the way you show up when no one is watching.

Why They Trusted Him

Pitsenbarger didn't have rank.
He didn't have authority.
He didn't have positional power.

What he had was **credibility** — the kind that comes from consistency.

The Army soldiers didn't know him personally.
But they trusted the type of Airman he was:

- disciplined
- calm
- competent
- selfless
- steady under pressure
- committed to the mission
- committed to them

Trust isn't about familiarity.
It's about reliability.

What He Did When He Hit the Ground

Once on the ground, Pitsenbarger moved through the chaos with purpose:

- he treated the wounded
- he pulled soldiers out of the line of fire
- he organized casualties for evacuation
- he redistributed ammunition

- he gave up his own gear
- he refused extraction
- he stayed with the soldiers as the firefight intensified

He didn't act like a visitor.
He acted like he belonged to them.

And when the helicopters were forced to withdraw, he stayed behind — not because he had to, but because **they trusted him, and he refused to break that trust.**

He was killed defending the men he came to save.

What Pitsenbarger Teaches Us About Trust

Trust isn't built by speeches.
It's built by **patterns**.

Pitsenbarger's leadership shows three truths about trust:

1. Trust is earned through competence

People trust leaders who know what they're doing — not because they're perfect, but because they're prepared.

2. Trust is earned through presence

He didn't lead from above.
He led from the ground — literally.

Trust grows when leaders show up where the work is.

3. Trust is earned through sacrifice

He didn't ask others to take risks he wouldn't take himself.

Trust deepens when leaders carry more than their share.

Why Trust Is the Final Week of Season 1

Everything in Season 1 leads to this moment:

- Clarity creates direction
- Listening creates connection
- Accountability creates fairness
- Belief creates confidence
- Hard conversations create honesty
- Humility creates approachability
- Integrity creates credibility
- Protecting what matters creates reliability

Trust is the **result** of all of them.

Trust is not a trait.
It's a consequence.

It's what people give you when your leadership has earned it.

The Cost of Leading Without Trust

When trust is missing, leaders don't lose influence instantly.
They lose it slowly.

You see:

- hesitation
- guarded communication
- minimal effort
- fear of risk
- lack of ownership
- compliance instead of commitment

People don't give their best to leaders they don't trust.
They give the minimum required to survive.

Trust is the difference between a team that performs and a team that endures.

The Quiet Strength of Leaders Who Are Trusted

Trusted leaders don't need to demand loyalty.
They don't need to remind people of their authority.
They don't need to perform confidence.

People follow them because they want to — not because they have to.

Trusted leaders:

- create safety
- create unity
- create clarity
- create stability
- create honesty
- create ownership

Trust is the force multiplier of leadership.
It accelerates everything.

Leadership Takeaway

Trust isn't built in the crisis.
It's revealed there.

Because the truth is simple:

When leaders earn trust in the small moments, teams stand with them in the big ones.

SEASON I REFLECTION — BECOMING

Season I was the season of beginnings — not the loud kind, but the honest kind.
The kind where you start seeing yourself clearly for the first time.

These early weeks weren't about mastery.
They were about awareness.
About noticing the cracks in your armor.
About understanding the difference between confidence and ego, between intention and impact, between leading and simply being in charge.

This season stripped away the illusion that leadership starts with others.
It doesn't.
It starts with you — your habits, your blind spots, your humility, your willingness to grow.

Season I was the moment you stopped performing leadership and started **becoming** a leader.

SEASON II

BREAKING / AWAKENING

There comes a point when the world stops letting you coast. When the easy lessons end and the real ones begin. Season II is about the moments that break you open — the failures, the shocks, the truths you didn't want but needed. These are the moments that wake you up and force you to grow.

WEEK 14

THE MOMENT THAT BREAKS YOU OPEN

"Growth begins the moment your confidence collides with reality." — Todd Fritz

The Fire That Forced NASA to Wake Up

On January 27, 1967, during a routine test on the launch pad, Apollo 1 caught fire. Three astronauts — Gus Grissom, Ed White, and Roger Chaffee — were killed in seconds. It wasn't a mission. It wasn't a launch. It wasn't even a high-risk moment.

It was supposed to be safe.

NASA was confident.
The engineers were confident.
The program was confident.

And then the fire exposed a truth no one wanted to see:

Confidence is not competence.
Momentum is not readiness.
And progress is not immunity.

The tragedy shattered the illusion that NASA's systems were as strong as its ambition. It was the moment the organization was forced to confront itself — honestly, painfully, and without excuses.

Season II begins in that same place.

The Leadership Lesson Hidden in the Fire

The Apollo 1 fire wasn't caused by one mistake. It was caused by **many small ones** — overlooked, minimized, or rationalized because the program was moving fast and success felt inevitable.

After the fire, NASA leaders had to face three truths:

1. They weren't as ready as they believed

The program had blind spots — not because people were careless, but because they were confident.

Breaking moments expose the gap between who you think you are and who you actually are.

2. They had stopped asking hard questions

Momentum creates comfort. Comfort creates silence. Silence creates risk.

Breaking moments force leaders to ask the questions they've been avoiding.

3. They needed to rebuild from honesty, not pride

NASA didn't defend itself.
It didn't hide.
It didn't blame.

It tore the program apart, examined every flaw, and rebuilt the entire system from the inside out.

Breaking moments demand humility — the kind that hurts before it heals.

Why Breaking Moments Matter

Every leader eventually hits a moment where:

- the plan fails
- the truth lands
- the weakness shows
- the illusion cracks
- the confidence collapses
- the world stops being polite

These moments feel like failure, but they're actually **inflection points** — the places where leaders either grow or retreat.

Breaking moments matter because they:

- expose what you've ignored
- reveal what you've outgrown
- confront what you've denied
- force what you've postponed
- sharpen what you've dulled

They are the moments that wake you up.

What Breaking Moments Do to a Leader

Breaking moments don't destroy leaders.
They **strip them down**.

They take away:

- ego
- assumptions
- shortcuts
- illusions
- comfort
- autopilot

And what's left is the truth — the real starting point of growth.

Leaders who avoid breaking moments stay shallow.
Leaders who face them become deep.

The Quiet Strength of Leaders Who Wake Up

After Apollo 1, NASA didn't collapse.
It transformed.

The fire became the catalyst that led to:

- safer spacecraft
- stronger engineering standards
- better communication
- more rigorous testing
- a culture that valued truth over speed

And two years later, that transformation put humans on the Moon.

Breaking moments don't end the story.
They rewrite it.

Leadership Takeaway

You don't grow when things go well.
You grow when something breaks — and you choose to face it instead of hide from it.

Because the truth is simple:

The moment that breaks you open is the moment that begins to build you.

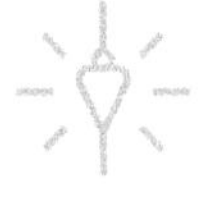

WEEK 15

THE MOMENT YOU REALIZE BEING RIGHT ISN'T ENOUGH

"Awakening begins when you stop assuming your truth is obvious to everyone else." — Todd Fritz

The Engineer Who Saw the Failure Coming

In the months leading up to the Challenger launch, engineer **Roger Boisjoly** warned that the Orings on the solid rocket boosters could fail in cold weather. He wrote memos. He raised concerns. He pushed the issue up the chain.

He wasn't guessing.
He wasn't speculating.
He wasn't being dramatic.

He was right.

But on January 28, 1986, Challenger broke apart 73 seconds after liftoff — exactly the failure he had predicted.

Boisjoly's awakening wasn't the moment the shuttle exploded.
It was the moment he realized something far more painful:

Being right doesn't matter if you can't make people listen.

The Leadership Shock Hidden in the Challenger Story

Boisjoly believed that truth would win on its own.
He believed that data would speak for itself.
He believed that expertise would carry weight.

But the Challenger disaster exposed a deeper leadership truth:

People don't act on what you know.
They act on what you make them understand.

This is the moment every leader eventually faces — the moment when you realize:

- your clarity wasn't clear enough
- your urgency wasn't urgent enough
- your influence wasn't strong enough
- your message wasn't heard the way you intended

It's the moment your confidence collides with reality.

What Boisjoly's Awakening Teaches Us

His story isn't about blame.
It's about the painful shift from **technical certainty** to **leadership responsibility**.

Three truths emerge from his experience:

1. Being right is not the same as being effective

Boisjoly had the correct analysis.
He didn't have the influence to match it.

Leaders learn — sometimes painfully — that truth without influence is noise.

2. People don't hear urgency unless you translate it

Boisjoly spoke in engineering terms.
Decision-makers heard "risk," not "catastrophe."

Leaders must speak in the language of consequences, not comfort.

3. Silence is not agreement — it's confusion

In the final launch meeting, hesitation was mistaken for consensus.

Leaders must surface doubt before doubt becomes disaster.

Why This Belongs in Season II

Season II is about the moments that break you open — the moments that force you to confront the gap between who you *think* you are and who you *actually* are.

Boisjoly's awakening is the same one every leader eventually faces:

- "I thought I was clear."
- "I thought they understood."
- "I thought the truth was obvious."
- "I thought expertise was enough."

It never is.

Season II begins when you stop assuming your message is landing and start taking responsibility for how it's received.

The Cost of Not Awakening

When leaders cling to the belief that "being right is enough," they experience predictable consequences:

- decisions drift
- risks compound
- communication fractures

- warnings go unheard
- teams operate on assumptions
- truth becomes optional

The cost isn't always as dramatic as Challenger — but the pattern is the same.

Leaders who fail to awaken repeat the same mistakes in different forms.

The Quiet Strength of Leaders Who Learn This Lesson

Leaders who awaken to this truth become different leaders:

- they communicate with clarity, not complexity
- they translate risk into reality
- they check for understanding instead of assuming it
- they build influence, not just expertise
- they speak up early, not loudly
- they refuse to let silence masquerade as agreement

They stop believing that truth is self-evident.
They start making truth unavoidable.

Leadership Takeaway

Being right is not the finish line.
It's the starting point.

Because the truth is simple:

Leadership begins the moment you realize your message isn't measured by what you say — it's measured by what others understand.

WEEK 16

THE DAY YOU BECOME "THEY"

"At some point in leadership, you stop saying 'they'—because you realize you are." — Todd Fritz

The Awakening No One Warns You About

Every organization has a "they."

"They changed the schedule."
"They made a new policy."
"They don't understand what it's like down here."
"They want us to do more with less."

When you're on the ground, "they" is everyone above you — the people who make decisions, set priorities, and shape the environment you have to live in.

And then one day, without ceremony or warning, you step into a role where the decisions are yours.

And the language shifts.

Not for you — for everyone else.

Suddenly, *you* are "they."

The Shock of Crossing the Invisible Line

The moment you become "they" isn't about rank or title.
It's about **impact**.

It's the moment when:

- your decisions ripple farther
- your words carry weight
- your silence gets interpreted
- your choices affect people you may never meet
- your intent matters less than your effect

It's the moment you realize leadership isn't about how you feel — it's about how your actions land on others.

This is the awakening that breaks you open.

Why Becoming "They" Feels So Heavy

When you're part of the team, you see leadership from the outside.
When you become "they," you see it from the inside — and the view is different.

Three truths hit fast:

1. You lose the luxury of simple opinions

It's easy to criticize decisions you don't have to make.
It's harder when the consequences belong to you.

2. You can't hide behind "someone else decided"

You *are* the someone else.
Your choices shape the environment others have to survive.

3. You realize how much you never saw before

The constraints.
The pressures.
The competing priorities.
The trade-offs no one talks about.

Becoming "they" forces you to confront the complexity you once dismissed.

The Leadership Danger of Forgetting This Moment

Leaders who forget what it felt like to be on the other side become:

- disconnected
- dismissive
- defensive
- insulated
- unapproachable

They start speaking in policy instead of people.
They start managing instead of leading.
They start believing their own explanations instead of listening to the impact.

The moment you forget you were once "us," you stop being worth following.

The Quiet Strength of Leaders Who Remember

The best leaders never fully leave the ground.
They carry their past with them — not as nostalgia, but as perspective.

Leaders who remember what it felt like to say "they":

- communicate with clarity
- explain the why, not just the what

- check their blind spots
- listen before deciding
- own the consequences
- stay human in the role

They don't run from the weight of being "they."
They honor it.

Because they know the people saying "they" are the same people they once stood beside.

Leadership Takeaway

You don't get to choose whether you become "they."
You only get to choose what kind of "they" you'll be.

Because the truth is simple:

Leadership begins the moment you realize the decisions you make are the ones others have to live with.

WEEK 17

WHEN YOUR IMPACT DOESN'T MATCH YOUR INTENT

"Leaders are judged by the wake they leave, not the story they tell themselves." — Todd Fritz

The Day a Leader Realizes Good Intentions Aren't Enough

Every leader eventually faces a moment that feels like a punch to the chest — a moment when someone tells you, directly or indirectly, that something you said or did landed wrong. Not because you meant harm. Not because you were careless. But because **your impact didn't match your intent**.

It's one of the most painful awakenings in leadership.

You think you're being clear — but someone feels confused.
You think you're being fair — but someone feels overlooked.
You think you're being direct — but someone feels attacked.
You think you're helping — but someone feels dismissed.

And the hardest part?

You don't get to decide how your leadership feels to other people.

That realization breaks you open.

The Punch You Never Saw Coming

Mike Tyson once said:

"Everyone has a plan until they get punched in the mouth."

He wasn't talking about boxing.
He was talking about **reality**.

Leaders walk around with plans, intentions, and internal narratives about who they think they are. But the moment someone tells you your impact missed the mark — that's the punch.

It's the moment your confidence collides with truth.
It's the moment your plan meets reality.
It's the moment you realize leadership isn't about what you meant — it's about what you caused.

That's the awakening.

Why This Awakening Hits So Hard

Leaders spend years building competence, confidence, and clarity. But none of that protects you from the moment someone says:

- "That's not how it felt."
- "That's not what I heard."
- "That's not what I needed."
- "That's not how it landed."

It's disorienting because it forces you to confront a truth most people never have to face:

Your internal narrative doesn't matter as much as your external impact.

This is where real leadership begins.

The Three Layers of the Impact Awakening

This moment doesn't just sting — it reveals blind spots you didn't know you had.

1. You realize your tone carries farther than you think

A leader's words echo.
A leader's silence echoes louder.

2. You realize people experience you, not your intentions

Intent lives inside you.
Impact lives inside them.

Leadership happens in the space between.

3. You realize your role amplifies everything

Once you become "they," your smallest actions feel big to everyone else.

This is the moment you understand the weight of the role.

The Danger of Ignoring This Lesson

Leaders who refuse to confront the gap between intent and impact drift into predictable patterns:

- defensiveness
- blame

- justification
- "they're too sensitive"
- "that's not what I meant"
- "they misunderstood me"

When leaders defend their intent instead of owning their impact, trust erodes quietly and permanently.

People stop bringing you the truth.
People stop giving you their best.
People stop believing you see them.

And once that happens, the title doesn't matter anymore.

The Quiet Strength of Leaders Who Learn This Lesson

Leaders who embrace this awakening become different leaders — deeper, steadier, more self-aware.

They start asking:

- "How did that land?"
- "What did you hear?"
- "What did I miss?"
- "What was the impact?"

They stop assuming clarity.
They start checking for understanding.
They stop defending their intent.
They start repairing their impact.

These leaders grow faster because they listen harder.

They don't crumble when confronted.
They get curious.
They get better.
They get trusted.

Leadership Takeaway

Your intentions shape your heart.
Your impact shapes your leadership.

Because the truth is simple:

Leaders aren't remembered for what they meant. They're remembered for what they caused.

WEEK 18

THE WEAKNESS YOU CAN'T OUTRUN ANYMORE

"Your strengths get you promoted. Your weaknesses decide how far you go." — Todd Fritz

The Moment You Realize the Problem Isn't 'Out There'

There comes a point in every leader's journey when the pattern you've been blaming on circumstances, personalities, or bad luck keeps showing up — even when the environment changes. Even when the team changes. Even when the job changes. And then it hits you. The common denominator is you.

Not in a self-punishing way. Not in a dramatic way. In a quiet, sobering, clarifying way. It's the moment you realize you're not being held back by the world — you're being held back by the part of yourself you've been avoiding. That's the awakening.

The Satya Nadella Moment

When Satya Nadella became CEO of Microsoft in 2014, the company was still powerful — but it was stuck. Innovation had slowed. Collaboration had fractured. Teams were competing internally instead of winning externally. The culture had become rigid, defensive, and territorial.

And Nadella realized something painful:

Microsoft's biggest weakness wasn't technical.
It was cultural.

And that weakness had followed the company for years — through reorganizations, leadership changes, and product cycles. It didn't matter how many brilliant engineers they hired or how many strategies they launched.

The weakness kept showing up because no one had confronted it.

Nadella couldn't outrun it.
He had to face it.

That was his awakening — and it's the same one every leader eventually reaches.

The Weakness That Follows You

Every leader has a weakness that trails behind them like a shadow:

- avoiding conflict
- over-controlling
- people-pleasing
- impatience
- perfectionism
- defensiveness
- indecision
- needing to be right
- needing to be liked

You can outrun it early in your career. You can hide it behind talent. You can bury it under effort. You can mask it with confidence. But eventually, the role gets big enough that your weakness steps into the light. And when it does, it doesn't whisper. It announces itself.

Why This Awakening Hurts

This moment stings because it forces you to confront three truths:

- **Your weakness is not new — your awareness is.** The flaw didn't suddenly appear. You finally stopped outrunning it.
- **Your strengths can't compensate anymore.** What used to be "good enough" is no longer enough. The role outgrew your shortcuts.
- **Your team already sees what you're just now admitting.** People experience your patterns long before you acknowledge them.

This is the moment when leadership stops being about performance and starts being about honesty.

The Story Every Leader Lives Through

There's a moment — sometimes small, sometimes seismic — when your weakness costs you something: a relationship, a decision, a moment of trust, a chance to grow, a chance to lead, a chance to be better.

It's the leadership equivalent of Tyson's punch in the mouth.

You had a plan.
You had confidence.
You had momentum.

And then your weakness showed up — and reality hit harder than your intentions.

That's the moment you stop running.

The Danger of Pretending Your Weakness Isn't There

Leaders who refuse to confront their weaknesses fall into predictable traps:

- blaming others
- repeating the same mistakes
- confusing motion with progress
- mistaking confidence for competence
- surrounding themselves with people who won't challenge them
- creating environments where truth becomes optional

Avoidance always becomes culture. And culture always becomes consequence.

The Quiet Strength of Leaders Who Face Themselves

Leaders who confront their weaknesses don't become perfect — they become trusted. They start naming the pattern, understanding the trigger, asking for feedback, building guardrails, slowing down when the weakness speeds up, choosing honesty over ego.

They stop hiding from the part of themselves that scares them.
They start shaping the part of themselves that leads others.

This is where maturity begins.

Leadership Takeaway

You can outrun a lot of things in leadership — pressure, conflict, discomfort, even truth. But you can't outrun yourself.

The moment you stop avoiding your weakness is the moment you start becoming the leader people hoped you were.

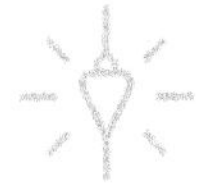

WEEK 19

THE MOMENT YOU REALIZE YOU BUILT THE PROBLEM

"You don't get the culture you want. You get the culture you make possible." — Todd Fritz

The Awakening Leaders Never See Coming

There's a moment in leadership that feels like a cold splash of water—the moment you look at your team and realize the issue isn't confusion, incompetence, or resistance. It's alignment. They're not doing the wrong thing. They're doing the thing your leadership made possible.

Not intentionally. Not maliciously. But predictably.

This is the moment you realize you didn't inherit the problem. You built it. And that realization breaks you open.

The Signals You Didn't Know You Were Sending

Leaders communicate constantly — not just with words, but with what they tolerate, what they ignore, what they reward, what they rush, what they delay, what they let slide, and what they never follow up on. Teams don't follow instructions. Teams follow patterns. And one day, you see the pattern clearly — and it looks uncomfortably familiar.

The Three Ways Leaders Accidentally Build the Wrong Behavior

- **You tolerated something once — and it became normal.** A missed deadline, a sloppy hand-off, a shortcut. You thought it was a one-off. Your team thought it was a standard.
- **You rewarded speed over quality — and now quality is gone.** You didn't say "rush." But your reactions said it for you. Teams listen to what you celebrate, not what you claim to value.
- **You avoided a hard conversation — and the problem grew teeth.** Silence is not neutral. Silence is permission. And permission becomes culture.

The Painful Realization

This moment hurts because it forces you to confront a truth most leaders avoid: you can't blame a team for following the rules you never enforced. It's not about guilt. It's about ownership. This is the moment when leadership stops being about managing others and starts being about managing yourself.

The Danger of Missing This Awakening

Leaders who never face this truth drift into predictable traps: blaming the team, tightening control, micromanaging, adding more rules, adding more meetings, adding more pressure. All of which make the culture worse, not better. Because the problem isn't the team. The problem is the system the leader unintentionally created.

The Quiet Strength of Leaders Who Own What They Built

Leaders who embrace this awakening don't collapse under the weight of it. They get sharper. They start resetting expectations, clarifying standards, repairing drift, having the conversations they avoided, modeling the behavior they want, and removing the behaviors they allowed. They stop blaming the team for following the path of least resistance. They start building a path worth following.

This is where transformation begins.

Leadership Takeaway

You don't rise to the level of your intentions. You rise to the level of your systems.

The moment you admit you built the problem is the moment you become capable of fixing it.

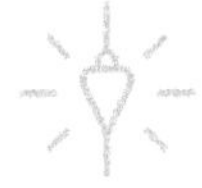

WEEK 20

THE MOMENT YOU REALIZE YOU HAVE TO DISAPPOINT PEOPLE

"Leadership isn't about keeping everyone happy. It's about keeping the mission healthy." — Todd Fritz

The Awakening Every Leader Tries to Avoid

There's a moment in leadership when you realize something you've been resisting for years: you cannot lead without disappointing people. Not because you're careless. Not because you're unkind. But because leadership requires choices — and choices create winners, losers, tension, and discomfort.

You can't approve every request.
You can't protect every feeling.
You can't satisfy every preference.
You can't avoid every conflict.

And the moment you finally accept that truth, something shifts inside you.
You stop trying to be the hero everyone loves.
You start becoming the leader your people actually need.

The Real-World Example: Tim Cook's First Hard Call

When Tim Cook took over as CEO of Apple, he inherited a company built on Steve Jobs' intensity, vision, and uncompromising standards. Cook was different — steadier, calmer, more operational. And early in his tenure, he faced a defining moment: Apple Maps launched in a rough, embarrassing state.

The world mocked it.
Customers were furious.
The press circled like sharks.

And Cook had a choice:

- protect the team
- protect the brand
- or tell the truth

He chose the truth.

He publicly apologized — something Jobs would never have done — and then made a painful internal decision: he removed the leader responsible for the product.

It disappointed people.
It upset people.
It shocked people.

But it also reset standards, rebuilt trust, and signaled something important:

Leadership isn't about avoiding disappointment.
It's about choosing the right disappointment for the right reasons.

Why This Awakening Hurts

Leaders who care — really care — struggle with this moment because it forces them to confront three truths:

- **You can't protect everyone from discomfort.** Growth requires friction.
- **You can't be fair to everyone in the way they want.** Fairness and agreement are not the same thing.
- **You can't lead if you're afraid of being misunderstood.** Clarity often feels like disappointment to someone.

This is the moment when leadership stops being about harmony and starts being about courage.

The Cost of Avoiding Disappointment

Leaders who try to keep everyone happy end up paying a price:

- standards slip
- accountability disappears
- resentment grows
- high performers leave
- low performers take over
- decisions get delayed
- culture drifts
- trust erodes

Avoiding disappointment doesn't protect people.
It protects dysfunction.

And dysfunction always sends the bill to the leader.

The Quiet Strength of Leaders Who Choose the Hard Thing

Leaders who embrace this awakening don't become harsh — they become honest. They start making decisions based on:

- mission
- values
- standards
- long-term health
- what the team *needs*, not what the team *wants*

They communicate clearly.
They explain the why.
They hold the line.
They stay steady when emotions rise.
They let people be disappointed without letting the mission be compromised.

They understand a simple truth:

Disappointment is temporary.
Clarity is lasting.
Trust is earned in the aftermath.

Leadership Takeaway

You can't lead without disappointing people — but you can disappoint people without disrespecting them.

The moment you stop trying to keep everyone happy is the moment you start leading with integrity instead of fear.

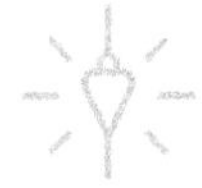

WEEK 21

THE MOMENT YOU REALIZE YOU CAN'T DO IT ALONE

"You can carry the title alone. You can't carry the mission alone." — *Todd Fritz*

The Moment the Weight Finally Hits You

There's a point in every leader's journey when the role gets too heavy to carry alone. Not because you're weak. Not because you're unprepared. But because leadership, by design, is bigger than any one person's capacity.

You can push through for a while.
You can grind.
You can muscle your way forward.
You can outwork the pressure.

But eventually, the truth catches up to you:

You can't do this by yourself.
And you were never meant to.

This realization doesn't break you.
It humbles you.
It opens you.
It matures you.

It's the moment you stop trying to be the hero and start building the team that can actually win.

The Real-World Example: Eisenhower Before DDay

In the months leading up to DDay, General Dwight D. Eisenhower carried the weight of the largest amphibious invasion in human history. The stakes were unimaginable. The risks were enormous. The consequences were global.

And yet, Eisenhower didn't pretend he could do it alone.

He built a team of commanders who were strong enough to challenge him, smart enough to disagree with him, and confident enough to bring him the truth — even when it was uncomfortable.

He delegated authority.
He trusted experts.
He listened more than he spoke.
He created space for dissent.

And when the final decision came — the moment to launch — he made it alone, but **he didn't arrive at that moment alone**.

Eisenhower understood something most leaders learn too late:

You can be accountable alone.
But you cannot be effective alone.

Why This Awakening Matters

Leaders who try to carry everything themselves eventually hit the same wall:

- burnout
- isolation
- decision fatigue
- tunnel vision
- resentment
- loss of perspective
- loss of trust

Trying to do it alone doesn't make you strong.
It makes you brittle.

And brittle leaders break.

The Signs You're Carrying Too Much

You know you're approaching this awakening when:

- you stop asking for help
- you stop delegating
- you stop trusting
- you stop listening
- you start believing "it's just easier if I do it myself"
- you start resenting the people you're supposed to be leading
- you start confusing control with competence

This is the moment when leadership stops being about effort and starts being about partnership.

The Quiet Strength of Leaders Who Ask for Help

Leaders who embrace this awakening don't become dependent — they become powerful.

They start:

- building teams that complement their weaknesses
- trusting people with real responsibility
- creating space for others to rise
- sharing information instead of hoarding it
- asking for input before making decisions
- letting go of the illusion of control

They stop trying to be the smartest person in the room.
They start becoming the leader who brings out the smartest thinking in the room.

This is where real leadership begins.

Leadership Takeaway

You can carry the title alone.
You can carry the accountability alone.
But you cannot carry the mission alone.

The moment you realize you can't do it alone is the moment you stop pretending you have to — and start building the team that can actually win.

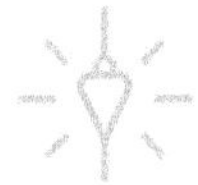

WEEK 22

THE MOMENT YOU REALIZE YOUR PRESENCE MATTERS

"You set the temperature of every room you enter — long before you speak." — Todd Fritz

The Moment You Finally See It

There's a moment in leadership when you walk into a room and notice something you never paid attention to before: the energy shifts. Conversations pause. Posture changes. People look up. Some straighten. Some shrink. Some relax. Some tense.

And you realize — maybe for the first time — that your presence carries weight.

Not because you're intimidating.
Not because you're important.
But because leadership changes the emotional temperature of every room you enter.

This is the moment you understand:

You're not just being watched.
You're being felt.

The Real-World Example: Mandela's First Cabinet Meeting

When Nelson Mandela became President of South Africa, the country was fractured, fearful, and uncertain. His first cabinet meeting brought together people who, months earlier, would never have sat at the same table.

And then Mandela walked in.

He didn't raise his voice.
He didn't assert dominance.
He didn't lecture.

He simply entered the room — calm, steady, composed — and the atmosphere changed.

People sat taller.
People softened.
People breathed.

His presence communicated something no speech could:

"You are safe.
We will do this together.
We will not be ruled by fear."

Mandela didn't lead with authority.
He led with presence.

And the room followed.

Why This Awakening Matters

Leaders often underestimate the power of their presence because they're used to being "just another person in the room." But once you lead, you're never "just another person" again.

Your presence communicates:

- safety or fear
- openness or judgment
- curiosity or certainty
- calm or chaos
- trust or suspicion
- respect or dismissal

People don't react to your words first.
They react to your presence.

The Signs Your Presence Is Shaping the Room

You start noticing:

- people wait for your reaction before giving theirs
- conversations shift when you enter
- people hold back when you're rushed
- people open up when you're calm
- people mirror your energy
- people read your silence as loudly as your words

This is the moment when leadership stops being about what you *say* and starts being about what you *signal*.

The Quiet Strength of Leaders Who Understand Their Presence

Leaders who embrace this awakening don't become performative — they become intentional.

They start:

- slowing down before entering a room
- checking their tone before checking their agenda
- listening before leading
- creating psychological safety
- modeling the behavior they want
- using presence as a tool, not a weapon

They understand that leadership isn't just about decisions.
It's about atmosphere.

And atmosphere is contagious.

Leadership Takeaway

Your presence is the first thing people experience and the last thing they remember.

The moment you realize your presence matters is the moment you start leading with awareness instead of accident.

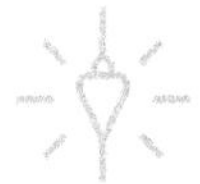

WEEK 23

THE MOMENT YOU REALIZE PEOPLE REMEMBER HOW YOU MADE THEM FEEL

"Long after your words fade, the feeling you left behind stays."
— Todd Fritz

The Awakening That Changes How You Lead

There's a moment in leadership when you look back on a conversation — maybe from years ago — and realize you don't remember the exact words, the exact issue, or the exact decision.

But you remember the feeling.

You remember whether you felt valued or dismissed.
Heard or ignored.
Respected or embarrassed.
Safe or judged.

And then it hits you:
Everyone you lead is having that same experience with you.

This is the moment when leadership stops being about communication and starts being about connection.

The Real-World Example: Mister Rogers in the Senate Hearing Room

In 1969, Fred Rogers — soft-spoken, gentle, unassuming — sat before a Senate committee ready to slash public broadcasting funds. The chairman, Senator John Pastore, was known for being blunt, impatient, and unimpressed by emotional appeals.

Rogers didn't match Pastore's energy.
He didn't raise his voice.
He didn't argue.
He didn't posture.

He spoke calmly.
He spoke sincerely.
He spoke with dignity and care.

And something remarkable happened.

The room softened.
Pastore softened.
The tension dissolved.

By the end, the senator — a man who walked in ready to cut millions — leaned back and said:

"I think you just earned the $20 million."

Not because Rogers delivered the best argument.
Not because he won a debate.
But because of **how he made the room feel**.

That's emotional leadership.
That's presence.
That's impact.

Why This Awakening Matters

Leaders often focus on:

- clarity
- direction
- standards
- decisions
- performance
- accountability

All important.
All necessary.

But none of it matters if people feel:

- belittled
- dismissed
- unsafe
- unseen
- unappreciated

People don't follow leaders they fear.
They comply.

People don't follow leaders who embarrass them.
They hide.

People don't follow leaders who ignore them.
They disengage.

But people will walk through fire for a leader who makes them feel:

- respected
- trusted
- valued
- believed in
- safe to speak
- safe to fail

- safe to grow

That's the difference between authority and influence.

The Signs You're Leaving Emotional Footprints

You start noticing:

- people remember your tone more than your message
- people repeat how you made them feel, not what you said
- people avoid you when you're rushed
- people open up when you're steady
- people mirror your emotional state
- people associate your presence with either tension or safety

This is the moment when leadership stops being about what you *intend* and starts being about what people *experience*.

The Quiet Strength of Leaders Who Understand Emotional Impact

Leaders who embrace this awakening don't become soft — they become intentional.

They start:

- slowing down before difficult conversations
- choosing tone before choosing words
- listening without rushing
- correcting without humiliating
- giving feedback without stripping dignity
- celebrating effort, not just outcomes
- creating emotional safety, not emotional distance

They understand that leadership is not just a cognitive act.
It's an emotional one.

And emotional leadership is what people remember.

Leadership Takeaway

Your words matter.
Your decisions matter.
But your emotional impact lasts the longest.

The moment you realize people remember how you made them feel is the moment you start leading with humanity instead of habit.

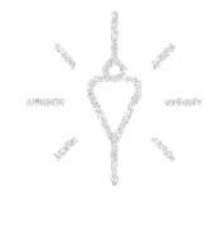

WEEK 24

THE MOMENT YOU REALIZE LEADERSHIP ISN'T ABOUT YOU

"Leadership begins the moment you stop trying to be impressive and start trying to be useful." — *Todd Fritz*

The Moment the Spotlight Finally Feels Wrong

There's a moment in every leader's journey when the attention, the praise, the credit — all the things that felt good early on — suddenly feel out of place. Not because you've lost confidence. Not because you've lost ambition. But because you've finally seen the truth:

Leadership isn't about elevating yourself.
It's about elevating the mission and the people who carry it.

This is the moment when the ego steps aside and the work steps forward.

The Real-World Example: Herb Kelleher at Southwest Airlines

Herb Kelleher, the legendary co-founder of Southwest Airlines, was known for something rare in corporate leadership: he refused to make himself the center of the story.

When the airline won awards, he credited the ramp crews.
When they hit record profits, he credited the flight attendants.
When they survived industry downturns, he credited the mechanics.
When asked about his leadership philosophy, he said:
"The business of business is people."

And he meant it.

Kelleher didn't try to be impressive.
He tried to be useful.

He wrote personal notes to employees.
He showed up at 3 a.m. to load bags.
He defended his people publicly and corrected them privately.
He made leadership about service, not spotlight.

And because of that, people didn't just follow him — they *loved* him.

Southwest didn't become the most profitable airline in history because of strategy alone.
It became that because its leader understood:

When leadership stops being about you, people start giving you their best.

Why This Awakening Matters

Leaders who make leadership about themselves eventually hit predictable walls:

- they burn out trying to prove themselves
- they become defensive when challenged

- they take credit and lose trust
- they confuse visibility with value
- they become the bottleneck instead of the multiplier

But leaders who shift the focus outward — toward the mission, the team, the work — unlock something far more powerful:

- loyalty
- creativity
- ownership
- initiative
- trust
- resilience

People don't thrive under leaders who need to be impressive.
They thrive under leaders who make *them* feel capable.

The Signs You're Still Making Leadership About You

You start noticing:

- you want to be the smartest person in the room
- you feel threatened when others shine
- you take on too much because you want the credit
- you talk more than you listen
- you feel the need to "prove" your value
- you measure your worth by visibility instead of impact

These are not flaws — they're signals.
Signals that you're still leading from ego instead of purpose.

The Quiet Strength of Leaders Who Make It About the Mission

Leaders who embrace this awakening don't disappear — they become clearer.

They start:

- giving credit away
- sharing the stage
- asking more questions
- listening longer
- celebrating others' wins
- removing obstacles instead of adding pressure
- focusing on outcomes, not optics

They understand that leadership isn't a performance.
It's a responsibility.

And the less they need to be impressive, the more impressive their leadership becomes.

Leadership Takeaway

The moment leadership stops being about you is the moment people stop performing for you and start performing *with* you.

The moment you stop trying to be impressive and start trying to be useful is the moment you become the leader people remember for the right reasons.

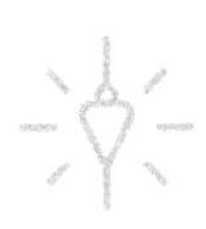

WEEK 25

THE MOMENT YOU REALIZE TRUST IS BUILT IN SMALL MOMENTS

"Trust isn't earned in the big moments. It's earned in the small ones when no one's keeping score." — Todd Fritz

The Awakening You Don't See Coming

There's a moment in leadership when you realize trust didn't come from the speech you gave, the decision you made, or the crisis you navigated. It came from the dozens of small, almost invisible moments that happened along the way.

The quick followup.
The honest answer.
The consistent tone.
The kept promise.
The quiet fairness.
The steady presence.

And suddenly it hits you:

**People don't trust you because of what you do once.
They trust you because of what you do repeatedly.**

This is the moment when leadership stops being about performance and starts being about pattern.

The Real-World Example: Coach Tony Dungy's Quiet Consistency

Tony Dungy wasn't the loudest coach.
He wasn't the most animated.
He didn't scream, throw clipboards, or use fear to motivate.

He led with calm.
He led with steadiness.
He led with consistency.

Players trusted him not because of one speech or one game, but because:

- he treated the star and the rookie the same
- he corrected without demeaning
- he praised without exaggerating
- he stayed composed under pressure
- he lived the values he preached
- he never changed his tone based on the scoreboard

Dungy built trust the same way great leaders do — **one small moment at a time.**

And when the Colts finally won the Super Bowl, his players didn't talk about the victory first.
They talked about the man.

Not the strategy.
Not the playbook.
The *man*.

Because trust is personal before it's professional.

Why This Awakening Matters

Leaders often think trust is built through:

- big decisions
- big speeches
- big wins
- big gestures

But trust rarely forms in the spotlight.
It forms in the shadows.

People trust leaders who:

- show up the same way every day
- follow through on the little things
- keep their word when it's inconvenient
- listen without rushing
- tell the truth without cruelty
- stay steady when others wobble

Trust is not an event.
It's a pattern.

The Signs You're Building (or Breaking) Trust

You start noticing:

- people relax around you
- people bring you the truth instead of the version they think you want
- people admit mistakes without fear
- people ask for help sooner
- people don't flinch when you give feedback
- people assume good intent instead of bad

Or the opposite:

- people hesitate
- people edit themselves
- people avoid you when something goes wrong
- people wait to see your mood before speaking
- people don't believe your "door is always open"

Trust is always being built — or eroded — in the smallest interactions.

The Quiet Strength of Leaders Who Understand This

Leaders who embrace this awakening don't chase dramatic moments.
They focus on the daily ones.

They start:

- showing up on time
- answering honestly
- following through
- apologizing quickly
- giving credit freely
- being predictable in the best way
- choosing consistency over intensity

They understand that trust isn't earned by being extraordinary.
It's earned by being reliable.

And reliability is a superpower.

Leadership Takeaway

Trust doesn't arrive all at once.
It accumulates.

The moment you realize trust is built in small moments is the moment you start leading with consistency instead of theatrics.

WEEK 26

THE MOMENT YOU REALIZE YOUR IMPACT IS BIGGER THAN YOU THINK

"A leader rarely sees the full reach of their influence — until the moment they have to step away." — Todd Fritz

There are moments in leadership that shake you in ways you don't expect.
Not because of crisis.
Not because of conflict.
But because of clarity — the kind that arrives when you're forced to confront what you mean to the people you serve.

I learned this during a season when a medical condition forced a hard conversation about my future in uniform. I had fought back with everything I had — discipline, training, fitness, grit — but the decision wasn't mine to make.

And now I had to tell my Airmen.

I expected disappointment.
I expected questions.
I expected concern.

I didn't expect what came next.

As the news spread, my phone lit up — texts, calls, emails, messages from people I had served beside for years. Some were from Airmen I worked with every day. Some were from people I hadn't seen in a long time. Some were from those who had moved on to other bases, other units, other chapters of their lives.

The messages were raw.
Unfiltered.
Human.

"Chief, don't leave us."
"Chief, I just reenlisted for six more years because of you."
"Chief, you're the reason I stayed in when things got hard."
"Chief, please fight this. We need you."

I sat there reading them, one after another, and something inside me shifted.

I had spent my entire career trying to pour into others — to steady them, guide them, push them, protect them, believe in them. I never once stopped to consider how deeply those efforts had taken root.

But now, in this moment of forced transition, I saw it clearly:

My words had mattered.
My presence had mattered.
My belief had mattered.
My leadership had mattered.

Not because I was perfect.
Not because I was special.
But because I showed up — consistently, quietly, and with purpose.

And now the people I had invested in were reflecting that investment back at me.

It was overwhelming.
Humbling.
Clarifying.

It reminded me of something leaders often forget:

We rarely see the full impact of our leadership while we're still leading.
We see it when we step away — or when we're forced to.

That moment taught me a truth I carry to this day:

Your influence is bigger than you think.
Your words reach farther than you realize.
Your presence shapes people in ways you may never fully understand.

And sometimes, the people you've led will remind you of your worth at the exact moment you need it most.

Leadership Takeaway:

Leaders seldom see their true impact in real time. Sometimes it takes stepping away — or being forced to — to understand how deeply your words and presence have shaped the people you serve.

SEASON II REFLECTION — BREAKING

Season II was heavier.
Sharper.
More honest than comfortable.

This was the season where pressure revealed truth — about you, about your people, about the cost of leadership.
You learned that influence comes with weight, and weight comes with responsibility.

You confronted the emotional side of leadership:
your reactions, your tone, your presence, your discipline.
You learned that people don't follow your words — they follow your regulation.
They follow your steadiness.
They follow the version of you that shows up when things get hard.

Season II broke the parts of you that needed breaking — the ego, the assumptions, the shortcuts — so something stronger could take their place.

This was the season where you stopped leading from instinct and started leading with intention.

SEASON III

REFINING

Once you've been broken open, you start to rebuild — intentionally this time. Season III is about refinement, clarity, and maturity. The lessons here are quieter, sharper, and more deliberate. This is where leadership becomes less about proving yourself and more about understanding yourself.

WEEK 27

THE MOMENT YOU REALIZE ACCOUNTABILITY STARTS WITH YOU

"A leader can't demand what they don't demonstrate." — Todd Fritz

The Shift From Awareness to Ownership

There's a moment in leadership when you stop looking outward — at the team, the mission, the circumstances — and you start looking inward.

Not with guilt.
Not with blame.
With responsibility.

You realize the culture you walk into every day is shaped by:

- your tone
- your habits
- your consistency
- your standards
- your follow-through

- your reactions
- your silence
- your example

And suddenly the truth becomes impossible to ignore:

Accountability doesn't start with the team.
It starts with the leader.

This is the moment when leadership stops being about expectations and starts being about embodiment.

The Real-World Example: Admiral William McRaven and the Bed

When Admiral McRaven gave his now-famous "Make Your Bed" speech, people laughed at first. A bed? Really?

But he wasn't talking about linens.

He was talking about discipline.
He was talking about standards.
He was talking about the smallest possible act of accountability—done consistently.

Because McRaven understood something most leaders miss:

If you can't hold yourself accountable in the small things,
you'll never hold others accountable in the big things.

His point wasn't the bed.
It was the pattern.

And patterns are what shape culture.

Why This Awakening Matters

Leaders who skip this moment fall into predictable traps:

- They demand what they don't model.
- They expect what they don't reinforce.
- They correct what they quietly tolerate.
- They blame the team for standards they never set.

But leaders who embrace this awakening unlock something powerful:

- credibility
- trust
- consistency
- alignment
- respect

People don't follow leaders who preach accountability.
They follow leaders who *live* it.

The Signs You're Owning the Standard

You start noticing:

- you correct yourself before correcting others
- you follow the same rules you enforce
- you stop making exceptions for your own behavior
- you apologize quickly
- you show up prepared
- you don't ask for effort you're not giving
- you don't hide behind the title

This is the moment when leadership stops being positional and becomes personal.

The Quiet Strength of Leaders Who Go First

Leaders who embrace this awakening don't become rigid — they become reliable.

They start:

- modeling the behaviors they expect
- setting the tone instead of reacting to it
- owning mistakes publicly
- reinforcing standards privately
- choosing consistency over convenience
- showing the team what "right" looks like

They understand that accountability isn't a tool.
It's a mirror.

And the leader has to look into it first.

Leadership Takeaway

You can't ask people to rise to a standard you don't live.

The moment you realize accountability starts with you is the moment your leadership becomes real — not because of what you demand, but because of what you demonstrate.

WEEK 28

THE MOMENT THE AIR LEAVES THE ROOM

When I took over as Chief, I inherited more than a squadron. I inherited its history — the good, the bad, and the forgotten.

In a storage closet, stacked against the wall, were three banker boxes filled with unissued service medals. Hundreds of them. Still sealed. Still waiting. Still unrecognized.

The explanation was always the same:

"Chief, there has been so many deployments we just haven't had time for ceremonies."

I remember staring at those boxes and feeling something settle inside me — not anger, not frustration, but a quiet conviction:

This isn't how we treat our people.

So we fixed it.
We issued every medal.
We restored every moment that had been overlooked.

But clearing the backlog taught me something else:

Recognition delayed is recognition diminished.

I needed a way to honor people in the moment — immediately, personally, meaningfully — even when the mission tempo didn't allow for formalities.

So I created the Iron Horse Award.

Not a coin.
Not a certificate.
Not a polished plaque.

Just a simple black wooden frame from a drugstore — less than five dollars — holding a printed picture of our mascot:

Charging Charlie.
The armored Red Horse.
Head down.
Shoulders forward.
Charging into the fight.

It wasn't fancy.
It wasn't official.
It wasn't approved by any board.

But it meant something.

Because it came from the Chief.
From their Chief.

And then came her.

A Dirt Boy.
One of the toughest, sharpest, most dependable Airmen in the squadron.
The kind who didn't complain.
The kind who carried more than her share.
The kind who brought healthy protein cookies to the shop because she wanted the team to stay strong.

At Commander's Call that afternoon, I presented her with the Iron Horse Award.

She lit up.

Not because of the frame.
Not because of the picture.
Not because of the cost.

Because it came from me.
Because it meant I saw her.
Because it meant she mattered.

She held it like it was something priceless.

And when the duty day ended, she walked straight to her car and called her sister to tell her about it.

That call changed everything.

The Next Morning

The next morning, she walked past my office carrying a container of her protein cookies — the ones she always made for the shop.

But something was wrong.

Her shoulders were slumped.
Her eyes were distant.
Her energy — normally bright, steady, grounded — was gone.

And her hands...
Her hands were trembling.

Chiefs know their people.
REDHORSE Chiefs have hundreds of Airmen, but we still know our people.

I stepped out of my office and said, quietly and casually:

"Good morning. Wonder if you could take a look at something for me..."

Not to alarm anyone.
Not to draw attention.
When a Chief speaks, people notice — so I kept it calm, subtle, private.

She followed me in.

I took the cookies from her hands so she wouldn't drop them.
I closed the door.
I turned to her.

And she broke.

Not loudly.
Not dramatically.

Quietly.
Completely.

Tears streamed down her face as she tried to speak.
Her breath shook.
Her voice cracked.
Her whole body trembled under the weight of something she had carried alone.

Between sobs, the words came out in pieces — fragile, broken, but honest.

"Chief... I was so excited... after Commander's Call... I... I called my sister."

I smiled gently, trying to steady her.
"That's wonderful. I'm sure your sister is very proud of you — just as I am."

That's when the dam broke.

A wave of tears.
Her breath catching.
Her hands covering her face as the storm overtook her.

I waited.
Silent.
Present.
Letting her feel what she needed to feel.

When she finally calmed enough to speak, she whispered the words that stopped the world:

"Yes... but no, Chief... she... she... my sister passed last year."

And the air left the room.

Reflection

I've carried that moment with me ever since.

Not because of the award.
Not because of the frame.
Not because of the ceremony.

But because of what it revealed.

Recognition is not about cost.
A five-dollar frame meant more than a fifty-dollar medal.

People break quietly.
The strongest Airmen often carry the heaviest loads.

Leaders must notice the small things.
A trembling hand.
A quiet walk.
A shift in energy.

Presence is the most powerful leadership tool.
Not speeches.
Not programs.
Not policies.

Presence.

The Iron Horse wasn't about the frame.
It wasn't about the mascot.
It wasn't even about the award itself.

It was about a moment of being seen.
A moment of pride.
A moment she wanted to share with someone she loved.

And that moment collided with grief she hadn't fully faced.

The Lesson I Carry Forward

Leadership isn't about ceremonies.
It isn't about medals.
It isn't about perfect timing or polished presentations.

It's about seeing people.

It's about recognizing them when it matters,
with whatever you have,
in whatever moment you're given.

That five-dollar frame didn't change her life.
Being seen did.
Being valued did.
Being recognized did.

And that's when I understood something I had missed for years:

Recognition is not a luxury.
Recognition is a lifeline.

People don't remember the cost of the award.
They remember the moment.
They remember the leader who noticed.
They remember the feeling of being valued in a world that often overlooks them.

The Iron Horse wasn't about the frame.
It wasn't about the mascot.
It wasn't even about the award itself.

It was about a leader saying:

"I see you.
I appreciate you.
You matter."

And sometimes that's the one thing holding someone together.

That day didn't teach me how to give awards.
It taught me why we give them.

Because recognition isn't about celebration.
It's about connection.
It's about humanity.
It's about leadership.

And the real Iron Horse?

It's every team member who keeps charging forward — quietly, humbly, relentlessly — carrying more than anyone realizes.

Our job as leaders is simple:

Notice them.
Honor them.
Stand with them.
And never let their effort go unseen.

WEEK 29

THE MOMENT YOU REALIZE PEOPLE ARE CARRYING MORE THAN YOU KNOW

"Everyone carries a weight you'll never see — and leadership begins when you choose to notice." — Todd Fritz

The Quiet Weight People Carry

There's a moment in leadership when you realize the people around you — the ones who show up, who grind, who smile, who push through — are carrying far more than you ever imagined.

Not because they're weak.
Not because they're struggling.
But because they're human.

And humans carry:

- pressure
- doubt
- responsibility
- financial strain

- family stress
- burnout
- fear of failing
- the weight of expectations

Most of it never shows.
Most of it never gets said.
Most of it never reaches the surface until something cracks.

And that's the moment leaders finally see it:

People are carrying more than you know — and more than they'll ever tell you.

The Real-World Example: The Strength You Don't See

In Japanese culture, there's a concept called *gaman* — a quiet form of endurance.
It means carrying hardship with dignity, patience, and self-control.
Not to hide pain.
Not to pretend everything is fine.
But to avoid burdening others.

People who practice *gaman* don't announce their struggles.
They don't broadcast their stress.
They don't ask for special treatment.

They show up.
They work.
They endure.
They carry their weight — and sometimes the weight of others — without letting it spill into the room.

A Japanese manager once described it this way:

"You can't tell who is struggling. The ones who look the strongest may be carrying the most."

That's *gaman*.
Quiet strength.
Invisible endurance.
A burden held with grace.

And it's everywhere — not just in Japan.

You see it in the employee who never complains.
In the teammate who always says "I'm good."
In the person who stays steady while others wobble.
In the one who carries responsibility without recognition.

The surface looks calm.
The weight underneath is enormous.

That's the lesson.

Why This Awakening Matters

Leaders who forget this truth become:

- impatient
- dismissive
- reactive
- judgmental
- blind to the quiet battles happening around them

But leaders who embrace it become:

- gentler
- more observant
- more patient
- more present
- more human

They stop assuming.
They start noticing.

They stop reacting.
They start understanding.

They stop demanding.
They start supporting.

This awakening doesn't make leaders soft.
It makes them accurate.

The Signs People Are Carrying More Than They Show

You start noticing:

- the smile that doesn't reach the eyes
- the shift in tone
- the slower walk
- the quiet withdrawal
- the sudden irritability
- the forced "I'm fine"
- the person who never asks for help

These are not weaknesses.
They're signals.

Signals leaders must learn to read.

The Quiet Strength of Leaders Who See the Invisible

Leaders who embrace this awakening don't pry — they pay attention.

They start:

- checking in privately
- asking real questions
- listening without rushing
- offering support without spotlight
- giving grace without lowering standards
- creating space for honesty

- noticing the small changes
- being present when it matters

They understand that leadership isn't about fixing people. It's about *seeing* them.

And sometimes being seen is the first step toward healing.

Leadership Takeaway

People rarely show you the full weight they're carrying.
But they always feel the weight of your presence.

The moment you realize people are carrying more than you know is the moment you start leading with compassion instead of assumption — and that changes everything.

WEEK 30

THE MOMENT YOU REALIZE LEADERSHIP IS LONELY FOR A REASON

"Leadership isn't lonely because you're alone. It's lonely because the weight is yours to bear." — Todd Fritz

The Truth No One Says Out Loud

There's a moment in leadership when you stop expecting the role to feel comfortable, social, or shared — and you finally understand:

Leadership is lonely for a reason.

Not because people avoid you.
Not because you're isolated.
Not because you're unsupported.

But because the role requires:

- seeing what others don't
- carrying what others can't
- deciding when others hesitate
- standing firm when others waver

- absorbing pressure so others can breathe

Loneliness isn't a flaw of leadership.
It's a feature.

The Weight of Being the One Who Knows

After Week 28's moment — the air leaving the room — and Week 29's awakening — realizing people carry invisible burdens — something shifts inside you.

You start to understand:

You're the one who sees behind the curtain.
You're the one who notices the tremor in someone's voice.
You're the one who reads the room before anyone else realizes there's something to read.

And that awareness comes with a cost.

Not a dramatic one.
Not a tragic one.
A *quiet* one.

The cost of clarity.

The Universal Example: The Lighthouse Keeper

Think about a lighthouse keeper.

They work alone.
They stand watch while others sleep.
They maintain the light no one sees up close.
They keep the lens clean, the flame steady, the signal constant.

They don't do it for recognition.
They don't do it for applause.
They don't do it for company.

They do it because ships depend on them —
even if the ships never know their name.

A lighthouse keeper once said:

"If I do my job well, no one notices. If I fail, everyone suffers."

That's leadership.

Not glamorous.
Not crowded.
Not shared.

Just steady.
Just responsible.
Just necessary.

And yes — lonely.

But lonely with purpose.

Why This Loneliness Matters

Leaders who fight the loneliness become:

- resentful
- insecure
- reactive
- approval-seeking
- inconsistent

Leaders who *accept* the loneliness become:

- grounded
- steady
- decisive
- clear
- trustworthy

Because they understand:

You can't lead from the crowd.
You lead from the edge.
You lead from the front.
You lead from the place where the view is different — and the responsibility is heavier.

That's why it feels lonely.

Not because you're unsupported.
But because you're accountable.

The Signs You're Growing Into the Role

You start noticing:

- you make decisions others don't want to make
- you carry information others don't have
- you protect people from pressures they never see
- you absorb conflict so the team can stay focused
- you stand alone in moments where consensus would be easier
- you feel the weight of the standard even when no one is watching

This isn't isolation.
This is leadership maturity.

The Quiet Strength of Leaders Who Accept the Loneliness

Leaders who embrace this truth don't withdraw — they stabilize.

They:

- stay calm when others panic
- stay objective when others get emotional

- stay steady when others shake
- stay accountable when others deflect
- stay present when others avoid

They understand that leadership isn't about being surrounded.
It's about being *centered*.

And sometimes the center is a very quiet place.

Leadership Takeaway

Leadership isn't lonely because you're alone.
It's lonely because the weight is yours to bear.

Leadership isn't about being alone.
It's about being willing to stand alone when it matters.

The moment you realize leadership is lonely for a reason is the moment you stop resisting the weight — and start carrying it with purpose, clarity, and strength.

WEEK 31

THE MOMENT YOU REALIZE NOT EVERYONE GETS ACCESS TO YOU

Leadership isn't about being everywhere.
It's about being where it matters.

The Shift You Don't See Coming

There's a moment in leadership when you realize something uncomfortable but necessary:

Not everyone gets access to you.

Not because you're better.
Not because you're distant.
Not because you're unapproachable.

But because leadership requires **discernment**.

Your time is finite.
Your energy is finite.
Your emotional bandwidth is finite.

And if you give everyone equal access, you end up:

- exhausted
- reactive
- scattered
- overwhelmed
- ineffective

Leadership isn't about being available to everyone.
It's about being available to the *right* ones.

The Difference Between Being Approachable and Being Accessible

Approachable means people feel safe coming to you.
Accessible means they can reach you whenever they want.

Those are not the same thing.

Great leaders are approachable.
Wise leaders are *selectively* accessible.

Because the moment you try to be everything to everyone, you become nothing to yourself.

The Chain-of-Command Technique (Week 4 Revisited)

Back in Week 4, we talked about your "chain-of-command" technique —the simple but powerful practice of teaching people to lead through the proper channels.

It wasn't about hierarchy.
It wasn't about ego.
It wasn't about control.

It was about **protecting your bandwidth** so you could lead at the right altitude.

Week 31 is where that lesson matures.

You start to understand:

If everyone can reach you directly, no one learns to lead.
If everyone can bypass the chain, the chain collapses.
If everyone can dump their problems on you, you stop being a leader and start being a sponge.

This is the moment you stop apologizing for boundaries —
and start enforcing them with clarity and confidence.

The Universal Example: The Gatekeeper at the Temple

In many cultures, temples have a gatekeeper — someone who stands at the entrance, not to keep people out, but to ensure the space inside remains sacred.

The gatekeeper decides:

- who enters
- when they enter
- how they enter
- and whether they're prepared to be there

They're not guarding a building.
They're guarding the **sanctity** of what happens inside.

Leadership is the same.

Your time is sacred.
Your clarity is sacred.
Your emotional stability is sacred.
Your decision-making space is sacred.

If you don't guard it, no one else will.

Why This Realization Matters

Leaders who fail to control access become:

- overwhelmed
- resentful
- reactionary
- distracted
- burned out

Leaders who master access become:

- focused
- steady
- intentional
- respected
- effective

Because they understand:

"My job isn't to be everywhere.
My job is to be where it matters."

The Signs You're Growing Into This Truth

You start noticing:

- you no longer respond instantly to everything
- you redirect issues back through the chain
- you protect your thinking time
- you stop letting people's urgency become your emergency
- you prioritize leaders who are actually leading
- you stop apologizing for boundaries
- you stop explaining your "no"

This isn't arrogance.
This is stewardship.

The Quiet Strength of Leaders Who Control Access

Leaders who embrace this truth:

- stay mentally sharp
- stay emotionally steady
- stay focused on the mission
- stay available to the people who truly need them
- stay aligned with their purpose

They understand that access is not a right —
it's a responsibility.

And responsibilities must be managed.

Leadership Takeaway

Not everyone gets access to you — and that's not selfish.
That's leadership.

Your time, your energy, and your clarity are finite.
Protect them.

**"Leadership isn't about being alone.
It's about being willing to stand alone when it matters." — Todd Fritz**

When you control who reaches you, you control what reaches you —
and that's how leaders stay steady at altitude.

WEEK 32

THE MOMENT YOU REALIZE YOU CAN'T TAKE EVERYTHING PERSONALLY

"If you take everything personally, you hand your peace to anyone willing to disturb it." — Todd Fritz

The Emotional Trap Every Leader Falls Into

There's a moment in leadership when you finally understand something that changes everything:

Not everything is about you — and if you treat it like it is, you'll drown in other people's storms.

People will project their stress, their fear, their insecurity, their frustration, and their unmet expectations. If you absorb all of that as personal attack, you lose your center. You lose your clarity. You lose your ability to lead.

This is the moment leaders learn one of the hardest truths:

You can't take everything personally — because most of it isn't personal.

The Jungian Truth: People Don't See You — They See Themselves

Carl Jung believed humans rarely react to reality. They react to their inner world.

He taught that people project their shadow, their wounds, their fears, their insecurities, and their unresolved conflicts onto others. You become the screen they project onto.

Jung said it simply:
"Everything that irritates us about others can lead us to an understanding of ourselves."

In leadership, this becomes:
Everything people throw at you often reveals more about them than about you.

When someone snaps at you, it's usually their stress.
When someone doubts you, it's usually their insecurity.
When someone criticizes you unfairly, it's usually their fear talking.

The mature leader learns to see the projection, not absorb the emotion.

The Samurai Truth: Fudōshin — The Immovable Mind

In Japanese martial tradition, there is a concept called *Fudōshin* — the immovable mind.

It doesn't mean emotionless.
It doesn't mean cold.
It doesn't mean detached.

It means unshakable.

A samurai trained not just to master the sword, but to master the self.
Calm when insulted.
Steady when provoked.
Centered when others try to pull them off balance.

Their power didn't come from force.
It came from discipline.

The moment you take things personally, you lose your center — and once you lose your center, you lose the fight.

Leadership is the same.

The Fusion: Jung Explains the Why. Fudōshin Teaches the How.

Jung teaches you:
This isn't about you.

Fudōshin teaches you:
Stay centered anyway.

Together, they form the leadership truth:
Understand the projection.
Control your reaction.

This is emotional mastery.
This is psychological altitude.
This is leadership maturity.

Why Leaders Must Learn This

Leaders who take everything personally become defensive, reactive, insecure, inconsistent, and emotionally exhausted.

Leaders who learn not to take things personally become steady, objective, grounded, emotionally intelligent, and respected.

Because they understand:
If I react to everything, I lead nothing.

The Signs You're Growing Into This Truth

You start noticing:

- You don't respond to tone — you respond to content.
- You don't assume intent — you ask for clarity.
- You don't internalize criticism — you evaluate it.
- You don't react to projection — you recognize it.
- You don't let someone's bad day become your bad day.
- You don't let praise inflate you or criticism deflate you.
- You stay centered even when others are spinning.

This isn't detachment.
This is discipline.

The Quiet Strength of Leaders Who Don't Take Things Personally

These leaders stay calm under pressure, stay objective in conflict, stay grounded in chaos, stay focused on the mission, and stay emotionally available without being emotionally hijacked.

They understand that leadership isn't about controlling others.
It's about controlling yourself.

And that begins with refusing to take everything personally.

Leadership Takeaway

Most of what comes at you isn't about you.
It's projection, fear, stress, or insecurity.

Your job isn't to absorb it.
Your job is to stay centered.

"If you take everything personally, you hand your peace to anyone willing to disturb it." —Todd Fritz

The moment you realize you can't take everything personally is the moment you stop reacting—and start leading with clarity, discipline, and strength.

WEEK 33

THE MOMENT YOU REALIZE CONSISTENCY IS MORE IMPORTANT THAN INTENSITY

"People don't need you at your best. They need you at your most reliable." — Todd Fritz

The Trap Leaders Fall Into

Early in leadership, intensity feels like commitment.

Long hours.
Big pushes.
Hero moments.
Late nights.
Visible sacrifice.

People notice it.
They applaud it.
They mistake it for strength.

But intensity has a flaw leaders don't see at first:
it depends on how you feel.

And when leadership depends on emotion, energy, or adrenaline, the team starts adjusting—not to the mission, but to *you*.

That's when leaders learn the hard truth:

Intensity impresses. Consistency stabilizes.

And stability is what people actually need.

The Trauma Nurse Who Never Changed Her Tone

In a Level1 trauma center, there was a charge nurse everyone wanted on shift.

Not because she was loud.
Not because she was fast.
Not because she brought intensity into the room.

But because **nothing about her changed when everything else did**.

Multicar pileup.
Gunshot wound.
Child trauma.
Masscasualty alert.

Her voice stayed level.
Her instructions stayed short.
Her movements stayed deliberate.

While others sped up, talked louder, and let urgency creep into their tone, she slowed the room just enough to keep it functional.

Doctors trusted her hand-offs.
New nurses mirrored her pace.
Veterans watched her for cues.

She didn't create calm.
She created **predictability**.

A resident once asked her how she stayed so calm under pressure.

She answered:

"I don't stay calm.
I stay *consistent*.
Calm is a feeling. Consistency is a choice."

In trauma care, unpredictability kills faster than lack of effort ever will.
People don't need energy.
They need **reliability**.

Why Intensity Breaks Teams Over Time

Intensity is emotional fuel.
Consistency is structural support.

Intensity fluctuates.
Consistency holds.

When leaders rely on intensity:

- Teams brace instead of trust
- People wait to see your mood
- Standards drift
- Stress spreads faster than clarity

When leaders rely on consistency:

- Decisions speed up
- Errors go down
- Confidence grows quietly
- People move without hesitation

Teams don't want a leader who can rise to the occasion.
They want a leader who **removes the need to rise at all**.

What Consistent Leadership Actually Looks Like

Consistent leaders:

- Show up with the same tone on good days and bad
- Enforce standards even when tired
- Make decisions the same way under pressure as they do in calm
- Correct without emotion
- Praise without exaggeration
- Stay predictable in the best possible way

This isn't boring leadership.
This is **functional leadership**.

And function is what saves people, missions, and teams when pressure shows up.

The Quiet Test of Maturity

Every leader eventually has to decide:

Do you want to be remembered for:

- The moments you burned hot, or
- The standard you held every day?

Because when people look back, they don't talk about how intense you were.

They talk about whether:

- You were fair
- You were steady
- You were reliable
- You were the same person when things got hard

Consistency doesn't feel heroic in the moment.

But it's the reason teams keep moving when everything else shakes.

Leadership Takeaway

Intensity creates moments.
Consistency creates trust.

Your people don't need more energy from you.
They need more **reliability**.

Because in the moments that matter most, no one asks:
"Did the leader care enough?"

They ask:
"Can we count on them?"

And that answer is built one consistent decision at a time.

WEEK 34

THE MOMENT YOU REALIZE CLARITY IS KINDNESS

"Unclear expectations don't make you nice. They make people anxious." — *Todd Fritz*

The Leadership Lie We Tell Ourselves

There's a moment in leadership when you finally understand something that changes how you communicate forever:

Being vague doesn't protect people.
It confuses them.

Being indirect doesn't spare feelings.
It creates anxiety.

Being "nice" at the expense of clarity isn't kindness.
It's avoidance.

Leaders often soften their words because they don't want to hurt someone, disappoint someone, or create tension. But the truth is simple:

Clarity is kindness.
Confusion is cruelty.

The Example That Makes It Obvious

For most of human history, microscopic life existed all around us — in water, in soil, on our hands, in the air. It shaped our world, our health, our survival.

But no one knew it was there.

Not because it didn't exist.
But because we didn't have the clarity to see it.

Then someone invented the microscope.

And suddenly, what had always been true became visible.

Leadership clarity works the same way.

Expectations, standards, responsibilities, and performance issues don't magically appear when you finally talk about them. They were always there — shaping the team, influencing behavior, affecting outcomes.

Clarity doesn't create truth.
Clarity reveals it.

And once people can see what's expected, they can finally act on it.

Then comes the part leaders don't like to admit:

It's hard to comply with a standard that was never clarified — but it's even harder to enforce.

You can't hold people accountable for something they didn't know they were supposed to do.
And you can't be surprised when they fall short of expectations you never made visible.

Without clarity, people aren't failing.
They're guessing.
And guessing is exhausting.

Why Clarity Matters More Than Comfort

People can handle hard news.
People can handle high standards.
People can handle accountability.

What people can't handle is uncertainty.

Unclear expectations create anxiety, hesitation, second-guessing, misalignment, frustration, and wasted effort.

Clear expectations create confidence, direction, trust, speed, ownership, and psychological safety.

Clarity isn't harsh.
Clarity is humane.

The Cost of Being "Nice" Instead of Being Clear

When leaders avoid clarity, they think they're protecting someone's feelings.
But what they're really doing is protecting their own comfort.

Avoiding clarity leads to misunderstandings, resentment, performance issues, unnecessary conflict, emotional distance, and broken trust.

People would rather hear the truth than live in uncertainty.

Unclear leadership forces people to guess — and guessing is exhausting.

The Power of Direct, Respectful Communication

Clear communication doesn't mean blunt.
It doesn't mean cold.
It doesn't mean unfiltered.

It means direct, respectful, honest, specific, timely, and actionable.

Clarity is not about tone.
Clarity is about responsibility.

Leaders owe their people the truth — delivered with dignity.

Why Leaders Avoid Clarity

Leaders avoid clarity because they don't want to disappoint someone, be the "bad guy," face conflict, trigger emotion, be misunderstood, or be disliked.

But leadership isn't about being liked.
Leadership is about being trustworthy.

And trust is built on clarity.

The Signs You're Growing Into This Truth

You start noticing:

- you say what needs to be said, not what's easiest
- you communicate expectations early, not after problems arise
- you give feedback directly, not through hints
- you stop sugarcoating and start explaining
- you choose honesty over comfort
- you stop apologizing for clarity
- you realize people appreciate directness more than you expected

This isn't harshness.
This is maturity.

The Leaders People Trust

People trust leaders who say what they mean, mean what they say, don't change the rules mid-game, don't hide expectations, don't leave people guessing, don't weaponize ambiguity, and don't confuse kindness with avoidance.

Clarity builds confidence.
Confidence builds trust.
Trust builds teams.

Leadership Takeaway

Clarity is kindness.
Confusion is cruelty.

People don't need you to soften the truth.
They need you to reveal it — the way a microscope reveals what was always there.

The moment you realize clarity is kindness is the moment you stop avoiding hard conversations — and start leading with honesty, courage, and integrity.

WEEK 35

THE MOMENT YOU REALIZE NOT EVERYONE GETS A VOTE

"Leadership isn't a democracy. It's a responsibility." — Todd Fritz

The Moment Every Leader Eventually Faces

There comes a point in leadership when you finally understand something that frees you, focuses you, and matures you:

Not everyone gets a vote.

Not everyone gets to influence your decisions.
Not everyone gets to shape your priorities.
Not everyone gets to weigh in on your direction.
Not everyone gets to sit at the table.

And that's not arrogance.
That's leadership.

Because leadership isn't about pleasing everyone.
It's about serving the mission and the people — in that order.

The Real-World Example That Shows the Magnitude

During one of my REDHORSE (Rapid Engineer Deployable Heavy Operational Repair Squadron Engineers) deployments in a contested area, our squadron got the green light to stand up a forward operating location — a bare-base airfield — in under 96 hours.

This wasn't a construction project.
This was a **strategic requirement**.

Fighter squadrons needed to generate sorties for close air support.
Medevac birds needed a safe strip to extract the wounded.
Tankers needed a place to refuel strike packages mid-mission.

Without that runway online, air dominance in the AO (Area of Operations) was at risk.
No persistent presence overhead.
No rapid response to ground threats.
No way to project power or sustain the fight.

REDHORSE doesn't just pour concrete.
We deliver the capability that lets the US Air Force and its allies own the skies.

We clear routes through denied terrain.
We sweep for IEDs (Improvised Explosive Devices).
We conduct demolitions to shape the battlefield.
We secure CLPs (Convoy Logistics Patrols) so fuel, ammo, and parts reach the front.
Every task carries life-or-death weight.

That afternoon in the TOC (Tactical Operations Center), two of my most experienced senior NCOs were locked in a heated standoff.

One argued we had to prioritize the runway pour immediately — get jets landing and launching or ground forces would be hanging without air cover.

The other argued we needed to divert heavy equipment to harden perimeter berms first — intel showed indirect fire incoming, and a single mortar could crater the fresh pour, kill the team, and destroy irreplaceable equipment.

Both were right in their lane.
Both were battle-proven.

I listened.
I pulled threat intel.
I ran timelines against the ATO (Air Tasking Order).
Together we weighed what failure in either direction meant:

No runway = no air dominance and unsupported troops bleeding out.
No protection = catastrophic losses and mission abort.

Then I made the call - neither had pitched.

We split the force smartly — accelerating the runway under lights and night ops while simultaneously building berms that shielded the pour site and the team. Rolling security bought us time and space.

It wasn't popular.
One NCO walked out shaking his head.
The other muttered about splitting focus.

But the first fighters touched down ahead of schedule.
When the mortars came, they hit dirt instead of people.
Medevac birds got the wounded out.
The air campaign stayed on rails.

Later, one of them asked, "Chief, why didn't you go with the majority opinion?"

I told him the truth:

"Because the responsibility doesn't fall on the majority. It falls on the leader."

That's the moment leaders grow up.

You can gather input.
You can respect expertise.
But responsibility isn't democratic.
It's singular.

And in a combat engineer unit a singular decision can enable everything from air dominance to keeping the fight supplied and alive.

The Trap of Trying to Make Everyone Happy

New leaders often fall into the same trap:

They want to be fair.
They want to be liked.
They want to be inclusive.
They want to hear everyone out.

Those are good instincts — until they become paralyzing.

When you try to give everyone a vote, you end up with:

- watered-down decisions
- endless debates
- emotional exhaustion
- unclear priorities
- slow execution
- frustrated teams

Consensus feels kind.
But it's often cowardice in disguise.

Why Not Everyone Gets a Vote

Because not everyone:

- sees the full picture
- carries the responsibility
- understands the constraints

- knows the mission
- feels the consequences
- bears the accountability

Leadership requires perspective.
Perspective requires altitude.
Altitude requires responsibility.

And responsibility is not evenly distributed.

The Difference Between Input and Influence

Great leaders listen widely — but decide narrowly.

Input is welcome.
Influence is earned.

People earn influence through:

- competence
- character
- consistency
- trust
- alignment with the mission
- demonstrated judgment

Everyone gets a voice.
But not everyone gets a vote.

The Weight of the Final Decision

When the decision is made, the leader is the one who:

- signs their name
- carries the consequences
- absorbs the criticism
- protects the team
- owns the outcome

That's why the leader gets the final vote.

Not because they're better.
But because they're responsible.

The Signs You're Growing Into This Truth

You start noticing:

- you stop chasing universal approval
- you stop letting loud voices outweigh wise ones
- you stop apologizing for making decisions
- you stop explaining yourself to people who aren't accountable
- you stop letting opinions dilute clarity
- you start trusting your judgment
- you start valuing alignment over agreement

This isn't ego.
This is maturity.

The Leaders People Follow

People don't follow leaders who try to please everyone.
They follow leaders who:

- listen
- decide
- communicate
- execute
- stand firm
- take responsibility
- move forward

Clarity builds trust.
Decisiveness builds momentum.
Responsibility builds respect.

Leadership Takeaway

Not everyone gets a vote.
Not because their voice doesn't matter — but because the mission does.

Leadership isn't about collecting opinions.
It's about making decisions.

The moment you realize not everyone gets a vote is the moment you stop leading by committee — and start leading with clarity, courage, and conviction.

WEEK 36

THE MOMENT YOU REALIZE ASSUMPTIONS DESTROY TRUST

"Assumptions are the stories we tell ourselves when we're too afraid or too busy to ask for the truth." — Todd Fritz

The Silent Killer of Teams

There's a moment in leadership when you finally understand something that changes how you communicate, how you listen, and how you lead:

Assumptions destroy trust.

Not because they're always wrong.
But because they're almost never verified.

Assumptions fill the space where clarity should live.
They create distance where connection should exist.
They generate conflict where none was needed.

And the worst part?

Most assumptions feel true in the moment.

The Example That Shows How Costly Assumptions Can Be

In 2003, a support convoy moving near Nasiriyah was told the route ahead was "secure." That assessment wasn't based on verified intel — it was based on **assumptions**.

Leaders assumed the area had been fully cleared.
They assumed the enemy had withdrawn.
They assumed the route was safe for soft-skinned vehicles.
They assumed no organized resistance remained.

None of it was confirmed.

As the convoy approached the city, they took a wrong turn — a turn that should have triggered questions, checks, or challenges. But everyone assumed someone else was tracking navigation. They assumed silence meant agreement. They assumed if something was wrong, someone would speak up.

Those assumptions stacked on each other — and the convoy drove straight into a coordinated ambush.

RPGs (Rocket Propelled Grenades) slammed into vehicles.
Small-arms fire erupted from alleys and rooftops.
Engines died.
Trucks burned.
Marines and soldiers were hit, isolated, or captured.
The mission collapsed in minutes.

And yet — in the middle of chaos — Marines fought block by block to extract survivors, pulling each other out of burning vehicles, returning fire, and refusing to leave anyone behind.

The failure wasn't courage.
It wasn't training.
It wasn't capability.

It was **unquestioned assumptions**.

Assumptions don't just break trust.
They break missions.

And when the cost is measured in lives, the lesson becomes permanent.

Why Leaders Fall Into the Assumption Trap

Leaders assume because:

- they're busy
- they're confident in their read of people
- they've seen similar situations before
- they think they "already know"
- they don't want to look uninformed
- they don't want to ask a hard question
- they don't want to slow down

But assumptions are shortcuts — and shortcuts cut trust.

The Discipline of Verification

Great leaders don't assume.
They **verify**.

Verification is:

- asking the extra question
- checking the source
- clarifying the intent
- confirming the expectation
- validating the information
- slowing down long enough to get it right

Verification isn't doubt.
Verification is respect.

The Emotional Maturity Behind "Help Me Understand"

One of the most powerful phrases a leader can use is:

"Help me understand."

It signals humility.
It signals curiosity.
It signals respect.
It signals that you value truth over ego.

And it prevents the single most common leadership failure:

Reacting to a story you created instead of the reality you never asked about.

The Signs You're Growing Into This Truth

You start noticing:

- you ask before reacting
- you clarify before concluding
- you check your story before believing it
- you stop assuming intent from tone
- you stop filling silence with suspicion
- you stop letting your past dictate your interpretation of the present
- you realize most people aren't malicious — they're human

This isn't softness.
This is discipline.

The Leaders People Trust

People trust leaders who:

- ask
- listen
- verify

- clarify
- communicate
- stay curious
- stay humble

Assumptions create distance.
Curiosity creates connection.
Verification creates trust.

Leadership Takeaway

Assumptions destroy trust.
Not because they're always wrong — but because they're rarely confirmed.

People don't need you to be psychic.
They need you to be present.

The moment you realize assumptions destroy trust is the moment you stop reacting to the stories in your head — and start leading with clarity, humility, and truth.

WEEK 37

THE MOMENT YOU REALIZE YOUR WORDS CARRY MORE WEIGHT THAN YOU THINK

"Your words weigh more than you think — because others carry them differently than you do." — Todd Fritz

The Moment You Finally Understand

There's a moment in leadership when you realize something that changes the way you speak forever:

Your words weigh more than you think.

Not because you're louder.
Not because you're smarter.
But because people attach meaning, urgency, and intent to what leaders say — even when you don't.

A casual comment becomes a task.
A suggestion becomes a requirement.
A question becomes a mandate.

A frustration becomes a warning.
A joke becomes a judgment.

Leadership amplifies your voice — whether you want it to or not.

The Example That Shows the Weight of a Leader's Words

On March 27, 1977, at Los Rodeos Airport in Tenerife, two Boeing 747s — KLM and Pan Am — found themselves on the same fog-covered runway due to a series of delays, diversions, and miscommunications.

The KLM captain was one of the most respected pilots in the world. Instructor. Check airman. A legend in the company.

And that's what made his words so heavy.

As the fog thickened and pressure mounted, the captain said to his crew:

"We're going."

He didn't shout it.
He didn't bark it.
He didn't issue it as a formal command.

But to the first officer and flight engineer — both junior to him — those words carried the weight of absolute authority.

Even though:

- they hadn't received takeoff clearance
- the runway wasn't confirmed clear
- radio calls were overlapping
- Pan Am was still taxiing ahead of them

The first officer hesitated.
The flight engineer questioned the decision.
But the captain's tone — confident, decisive, impatient — overrode their instincts.

Because when a leader speaks, subordinates don't hear "opinion." They hear **direction**.

The KLM 747 accelerated down the runway.
The Pan Am 747 emerged from the fog too late.
The collision killed 583 people — still the deadliest aviation accident in history.

The investigation didn't blame skill.
It didn't blame malice.
It didn't blame incompetence.

It blamed **the weight of a leader's words**.

A single phrase — spoken casually, interpreted literally — became catastrophic.

Your intent doesn't travel with your words.
Only your impact does.

Why Your Words Hit Harder Than You Expect

People attach weight to a leader's words because:

- they want to meet your expectations
- they assume you see something they don't
- they believe your words reflect the mission's priorities
- they don't want to disappoint you
- they interpret tone as direction
- they take your comments personally, even when you don't mean them that way

Leadership magnifies everything you say.

The Unintended Consequences of Casual Comments

A leader's offhand remark can:

- derail priorities
- create confusion
- shift manpower
- spark unnecessary urgency
- cause emotional stress
- make people feel judged
- create fear where none was intended
- break trust without meaning to

People don't hear your words.
They hear your **position**.

The Discipline of Intentional Speech

Great leaders don't speak less — they speak **deliberately**.

Intentional speech means:

- thinking before you talk
- clarifying when you're brainstorming vs. directing
- labeling your thoughts ("This is just an idea...")
- being precise with expectations
- avoiding sarcasm that can be misinterpreted
- understanding the emotional climate before you speak
- recognizing that your tone sets the tone

Intentional speech isn't about being careful.
It's about being responsible.

The Emotional Maturity Behind "Let Me Clarify What I Meant"

One of the most powerful leadership phrases is:

"Let me clarify what I meant."

It resets expectations.
It removes confusion.
It prevents unnecessary stress.
It shows humility.
It protects trust.

Leaders who clarify aren't weak.
They're wise.

The Signs You're Growing Into This Truth

You start noticing:

- you pause before speaking
- you label your comments as ideas, not directives
- you check for understanding
- you correct misinterpretations quickly
- you stop venting downward
- you stop joking at someone's expense
- you realize people react to your tone, not just your words
- you understand that silence can be interpreted too

This isn't caution.
This is maturity.

The Leaders People Trust

People trust leaders who:

- communicate clearly
- speak with purpose
- correct misunderstandings
- avoid careless comments
- use their voice to build, not break
- understand the weight of their influence

Your words can steady a team — or shake it.

Leadership Takeaway

Your words carry more weight than you think.
Not because of who you are — but because of what your position means to others.

People don't need you to be perfect.
They need you to be intentional.

The moment you realize your words carry weight is the moment you stop speaking casually — and start communicating like a leader.

WEEK 38

THE MOMENT YOU REALIZE ACCOUNTABILITY ISN'T ABOUT BLAME

"Accountability is ownership. Blame is avoidance dressed up as leadership." — Todd Fritz

The Moment You Finally Understand

There's a moment in leadership when you realize something that changes how you handle mistakes, conflict, and performance forever:

Accountability isn't about blame.

Blame is emotional.
Blame is reactive.
Blame is loud.
Blame is easy.

Accountability is different.

Accountability is calm.
Accountability is deliberate.

Accountability is responsible.
Accountability is mature.

Blame looks backward.
Accountability looks forward.

Blame punishes.
Accountability improves.

Blame divides.
Accountability unites.

The Example That Shows the Difference

In 2010, a major U.S. Navy cruiser ran aground near the port of Dubai. No enemy fire. No mechanical failure. No catastrophic weather. Just a navigational error during a routine approach.

The immediate reaction from outside observers was predictable:

"Who screwed up?"
"Who's at fault?"
"Who do we fire?"

But inside the Navy, something different happened.

The commanding officer didn't blame the junior officer on the helm.
He didn't blame the navigator.
He didn't blame the watch team.
He didn't blame the charts, the tide, or the equipment.

He said:

**"I own this.
If my team wasn't aligned, trained, or supported well enough to prevent this, that's on me."**

That wasn't weakness.
That was leadership.

Because accountability isn't about pointing fingers.
It's about holding the mirror.

The investigation later showed multiple small breakdowns — communication gaps, assumption chains, and missed crosschecks. But the CO's response set the tone:

We don't fix problems by hunting villains.
We fix problems by understanding them.

That's accountability.

Why Blame Feels Good — and Why It Fails

Blame gives leaders:

- a quick emotional release
- a sense of control
- a target for frustration
- a way to look decisive
- a way to protect their ego

But blame destroys:

- trust
- initiative
- honesty
- psychological safety
- team cohesion

Blame teaches people to hide mistakes instead of surface them.

And hidden mistakes don't disappear — they grow.

What Accountability Actually Looks Like

Accountability is:

- identifying the root cause
- owning your part
- clarifying expectations
- improving systems
- coaching people
- preventing recurrence
- strengthening the team

Accountability is not:

- humiliation
- punishment
- public shaming
- emotional outbursts
- scapegoating
- fear-based leadership

Accountability is a process.
Blame is a reaction.

The Emotional Maturity Behind "This One's On Me"

One of the most powerful phrases a leader can use is:

"This one's on me."

Not as a shield.
Not as a performance.
Not as martyrdom.

But as a signal:

- I'm not here to punish you
- I'm here to protect the mission
- I'm here to learn
- I'm here to lead

When leaders own outcomes, teams follow them anywhere.

When leaders blame others, teams follow them nowhere.

The Signs You're Growing Into This Truth

You start noticing:

- you respond instead of react
- you ask questions instead of accuse
- you focus on systems, not scapegoats
- you look for causes, not culprits
- you protect your people instead of exposing them
- you coach instead of criticize
- you own the outcome even when you didn't cause the problem

This isn't softness.
This is strength.

The Leaders People Trust

People trust leaders who:

- take responsibility
- stay calm under pressure
- protect their team
- correct without humiliating
- learn from mistakes
- improve processes
- model humility

Accountability builds trust.
Blame destroys it.

Leadership Takeaway

Accountability isn't about blame.
Blame is emotional.
Accountability is intentional.

People don't need a leader who hunts for fault.
They need a leader who builds a path forward.

The moment you realize accountability isn't about blame is the moment you stop reacting to mistakes — and start leading your team through them.

WEEK 39

THE MOMENT YOU REALIZE STANDARDS DON'T LOWER THEMSELVES

"Standards don't slip all at once. They erode one unchallenged moment at a time." — Todd Fritz

The Moment You Finally Understand

There's a moment in leadership when you realize something uncomfortable but liberating:

Standards don't lower themselves.
Leaders lower them — usually by accident.

Not through big decisions.
Not through dramatic failures.
But through small moments of silence.

The moment you let something slide.
The moment you look the other way.
The moment you tell yourself "just this once."
The moment you avoid a conversation because you're tired.
The moment you accept "good enough" because you're busy.

That's how standards fall.
Not with a crash — with a whisper.

The Example That Shows How Standards Erode

In 2014, a major U.S. fire department conducted an internal review after a series of preventable injuries during routine operations. What they found wasn't shocking — but it was sobering.

The issue wasn't training.
It wasn't equipment.
It wasn't staffing.

It was **drift**.

Over time, crews had slowly stopped wearing certain pieces of protective gear during "simple" calls. First it was gloves. Then hoods. Then eye protection. Then SCBA masks during overhaul.

Not because they were lazy.
Not because they didn't care.
But because:

- the last call went fine
- the one before that went fine
- the one before that went fine
- no one said anything
- no one corrected it
- no one reinforced the standard

And when nothing bad happens, the brain rewires itself:

"If nothing went wrong, then it must be safe."

Until the day it wasn't.

A firefighter suffered severe burns during what should have been a routine mop-up. The investigation didn't blame the individual. It blamed the **culture of unchallenged drift**.

The chief said something every leader should tattoo on their soul:

**"We didn't lose our standards.
We abandoned them one quiet moment at a time."**

That's the truth.

Standards don't collapse.
Leaders allow erosion.

Why Standards Slip

Standards slip because leaders:

- avoid conflict
- assume people "know better"
- don't want to seem nitpicky
- get tired
- get busy
- get comfortable
- get distracted
- get complacent

But here's the truth:

Every unchallenged moment becomes the new standard.

The Discipline of Protecting Standards

Great leaders don't protect standards with speeches.
They protect them with **consistency**.

Consistency is:

- correcting small things early
- reinforcing expectations often
- modeling the behavior yourself
- refusing to let fatigue dictate discipline

- addressing drift before it becomes culture
- being fair, firm, and predictable

Consistency isn't glamorous.
It's leadership.

The Emotional Maturity Behind "We Don't Do That Here"

One of the most powerful phrases a leader can use is:

"We don't do that here."

Not angry.
Not dramatic.
Not demeaning.

Just clear.

It resets the standard.
It protects the culture.
It reinforces identity.

Leaders who protect standards protect their people.

The Signs You're Growing Into This Truth

You start noticing:

- you correct drift early
- you stop apologizing for enforcing standards
- you stop letting "busy" become an excuse
- you model what you expect
- you address small issues before they become big ones
- you understand that silence is approval
- you realize standards aren't rules — they're promises

This isn't rigidity.
This is responsibility.

The Leaders People Trust

People trust leaders who:

- are consistent
- are predictable
- enforce standards fairly
- don't play favorites
- don't let things slide
- protect the culture
- protect the mission

Standards are the backbone of trust.

Leadership Takeaway

Standards don't lower themselves.
They erode when leaders stop protecting them.

People don't need a leader who's perfect.
They need a leader who's consistent.

The moment you realize standards don't lower themselves is the moment you stop letting drift define your culture — and start leading with clarity, discipline, and integrity.

SEASON III REFLECTION — REFINING

Season III was quiet.
Not soft — quiet.

This was the season of maturity.
The season where leadership stopped being about you and started being about the people you serve.

You learned the difference between ownership and stewardship.
You learned that your emotional ceiling becomes everyone else's emotional ceiling.
You learned that the loud moments don't define you — the quiet ones do.

This season taught you that leadership isn't a spotlight.
It's a responsibility.
It's a trust.
It's a long game measured not in applause, but in continuity.

Season III refined you — sanded the edges, sharpened the discipline, deepened the humility.
It prepared you for the truths that only come at the end of a long road.

SEASON IV

LEADING

Legacy isn't about age or rank. It's about impact — the kind that outlives your presence. Season IV is where the lessons become distilled, universal, and deeply human. It's where leadership shifts from something you do to something you are. And it's where the journey comes full circle.

WEEK 40

THE MOMENT YOU REALIZE HESITATION IS A DECISION

"Your window to act is never perfect. Leaders move anyway."
— Todd Fritz

The Moment You Finally Understand

There's a moment in leadership when you realize something that changes how you make decisions forever:

Hesitation is a decision.
And in high-stakes moments, it's often the wrong one.

Leaders rarely get perfect clarity.
They get fragments.
They get pressure.
They get time working against them.

And yet — they must act.

Because waiting for perfect information is its own kind of failure.

The Example That Shows the Cost of Hesitation — and the Power of Decisive Action

On March 4, 2002, during the Battle of Takur Ghar, U.S. Air Force Technical Sergeant **John A. Chapman**, a Special Tactics Combat Controller, faced a situation that would define the meaning of decisive leadership.

A. The Initial Assault — Acting With Incomplete Information

Chapman and his team were inserted onto a ridge under heavy fire. They didn't know:

- how many fighters were entrenched
- where the enemy positions were
- whether the landing zone was compromised
- whether reinforcements were coming

They had **40–70% of the picture** — exactly the zone Colin Powell described as the decision window for leaders.

Chapman didn't freeze.
He didn't wait for perfect clarity.
He didn't stall for more intel.

He **moved**.

He charged uphill through deep snow, under machine-gun fire, clearing bunkers and creating space for his team to survive. His decisiveness — not certainty — is what broke the enemy's advantage.

He acted because hesitation would have meant death for everyone behind him.

That's leadership.

B. The Decision to ReEngage Alone — The Ultimate Example of Moral Courage

After being separated from his team, wounded, and alone on the ridge, Chapman regained consciousness.

He could have stayed hidden.
He could have waited.
He could have hoped someone else would act.

Instead, he **reengaged the enemy alone**, buying time for incoming forces, protecting aircraft overhead, and continuing to fight with full awareness of the risk.

He didn't have perfect information.
He didn't have support.
He didn't have certainty.

He had a window — and the courage to move through it.

Chapman's final stand wasn't just bravery.
It was decisive leadership under the harshest conditions imaginable.

He acted because **hesitation would have cost others their lives**.

The Powell 40–70 Rule — The Framework for Decisive Leadership

General Colin Powell taught that leaders should make decisions when they have **40–70% of the information**.

Less than 40% → you're guessing.
More than 70% → you're too slow.

Because by the time you have perfect clarity, the window is gone.

Chapman lived this truth.
He didn't wait for certainty.
He acted in the zone where leaders earn their pay — and their legacy.

The Double-Edged Sword of Decision Making

Leaders face two dangers:

1. Acting too soon

Recklessness.
Impulsiveness.
Ignoring risk.

2. Acting too late

Hesitation.
Paralysis.
Missed opportunity.

The mature leader lives in the tension between the two.

Decisiveness isn't about being fast.
It's about being **timely**.

Why Leaders Hesitate — and Why It's Dangerous

Leaders hesitate because:

- they want more information
- they fear being wrong
- they fear the consequences
- they want someone else to decide
- they hope the situation resolves itself

But hesitation:

- closes windows
- increases risk
- shifts initiative to the enemy
- creates confusion
- erodes trust
- costs lives

Hesitation is not neutral.
It is a choice — and often the most dangerous one.

The Discipline of Decisive Leadership

Decisive leaders:

- act with incomplete information
- accept uncertainty
- move when the window is open
- understand the cost of delay
- communicate clearly
- take responsibility for outcomes
- protect their people through action, not avoidance

Decisiveness is not recklessness.
It is responsibility under pressure.

The Emotional Maturity Behind "We Move Now"

One of the most powerful leadership phrases is:

"We move now."

Not because the leader is certain.
But because the leader understands:

- the window is closing
- the risk of waiting is greater than the risk of acting
- someone must decide

Leaders don't wait for perfect clarity.
They create clarity through action.

The Signs You're Growing Into This Truth

You start noticing:

- you make decisions earlier
- you stop waiting for perfect information
- you accept that uncertainty is part of leadership
- you understand the cost of hesitation
- you move when the window opens
- you take responsibility for the call
- you stop outsourcing courage

This isn't aggression.
This is maturity.

The Leaders People Trust

People trust leaders who:

- act when others freeze
- move with purpose
- accept risk honestly
- protect their team through decisiveness
- communicate clearly under pressure
- don't hide behind uncertainty

Decisiveness builds trust.
Hesitation erodes it.

Leadership Takeaway

Hesitation is a decision.
And in high-stakes moments, it's often the wrong one.

Leaders rarely get perfect clarity.
They get a window — and the courage to move through it.

TSgt John A. Chapman lived that truth.
And leaders who follow his example honor him not with words, but with action.

WEEK 41

THE MOMENT YOU REALIZE RESPECT ISN'T GIVEN TO YOU — IT'S RETURNED TO YOU

"No one owes you respect. Not your rank, not your title, not your position. Respect is returned to you based on how you lead." — *Todd Fritz*

The Moment You Finally Understand

There's a moment in leadership — usually later than you expect — when you realize something that changes the way you carry yourself forever:

People don't have to respect you.
They choose to.

Authority is assigned.
Respect is earned.

You can demand compliance.
You cannot demand respect.

And the day you understand that is the day you stop performing leadership and start living it.

The Moment Leaders Learn the Hard Truth

Every leader eventually faces the same realization:

People don't respect you because of your position.
They respect you because of your behavior.

You can walk into a room with authority.
You cannot walk into a room with respect.

Respect isn't automatic.
It isn't guaranteed.
It isn't tied to your title.

Respect is earned through:

- consistency
- fairness
- humility
- emotional steadiness
- how you treat people who can't do anything for you
- how you show up when things get hard

And here's the part most leaders don't want to hear:

If the people you lead don't respect you, your influence is already gone.

Not because they're rebellious.
Not because they're difficult.
But because respect is the foundation of trust — and trust is the foundation of leadership.

When people respect you, they follow you willingly.
When they don't, they follow you only because they have to.

And that's not leadership.
That's compliance.

Fear vs. Respect — The Line Weak Leaders Don't See

Weak leaders confuse fear with respect.

Fear looks like:

- silence
- compliance
- distance
- avoidance
- "yes, sir" with no conviction

Respect looks like:

- honesty
- initiative
- trust
- loyalty
- people bringing you problems before they explode

Fear gets you obedience.
Respect gets you commitment.

Fear collapses when you're not in the room.
Respect carries your influence even when you're gone.

How Respect Is Earned — And How It's Lost

Respect is earned through:

- consistency
- fairness
- humility
- owning your mistakes
- protecting your people
- enforcing standards evenly
- listening more than you talk
- being the same person on good days and bad days

Respect is lost through:

- ego
- emotional volatility
- hypocrisy
- favoritism
- weaponizing authority
- talking down to people
- blaming instead of owning
- disappearing when things get hard

Respect is slow to earn and fast to lose.

The Discipline of Leading With Respect

Leaders who earn respect:

- speak to people, not at them
- stay calm under pressure
- enforce standards without arrogance
- listen before deciding
- treat everyone with dignity
- admit when they're wrong
- show up when it matters
- never hide behind their title

Respect isn't about being liked.
It's about being trusted.

The Emotional Maturity Behind "I Don't Expect Respect — I Earn It"

One of the most powerful leadership statements is:

**"I don't expect respect because of my position.
I earn it through my actions."**

That's humility.
That's maturity.
That's leadership.

And people follow leaders who live that truth.

The Signs You're Growing Into This Truth

You start noticing:

- you stop assuming people owe you anything
- you listen more
- you talk less
- you treat everyone with dignity
- you enforce standards without ego
- you stop using authority as a shield
- you understand that respect is a reflection of your behavior
- you realize influence is earned, not assigned

This isn't softness.
This is strength.

The Leaders People Respect

People respect leaders who:

- are consistent
- are fair
- are humble
- are steady

- are honest
- are present
- are human

Respect is the foundation of influence.
Without it, nothing else works.

Leadership Takeaway

Respect isn't given to you.
It's returned to you.

Not because of your rank.
Not because of your title.
But because of how you lead.

The moment you realize respect is earned — not owed — is the moment you stop performing leadership… and start living it.

WEEK 42

THE MOMENT YOU REALIZE LEADERSHIP IS MEASURED BY HOW YOU HANDLE POWER

"Leadership isn't measured by how much power you have.
It's measured by how you handle the power you're given." — Todd Fritz

The Moment You Finally Understand

There's a moment in leadership — usually after you've earned trust, influence, and authority—when you realize something that separates mature leaders from everyone else:

Power doesn't change who you are.
It reveals who you are.

People don't watch how you act when you're struggling.
They watch how you act when you're in charge.

Because power is the ultimate Xray.
It exposes ego.
It exposes insecurity.
It exposes character.
It exposes discipline.

And it exposes whether you're a leader... or just someone who likes being in control.

The Quiet Test Every Leader Takes

Most leaders think they're being evaluated during crises, conflicts, or high-pressure moments.

But the real test happens in the quiet moments:

- when you could take credit
- when you could blame someone else
- when you could cut a corner
- when you could ignore a standard
- when you could use your position to get your way
- when you could talk down to someone and no one would correct you
- when you could get away with something simply because of who you are

Those moments reveal everything.

People don't judge leaders by how they act when things are hard. They judge them by how they act when they have **power**.

A Real Story — The Day Pixar's President Refused to Use His Power as a Weapon

During the production of *Toy Story 2*, Pixar was in trouble.
The film was behind schedule.
The story wasn't working.
The team was exhausted.
Morale was collapsing.

Disney leadership wanted heads to roll.
They wanted a public correction.
They wanted someone punished to "send a message."

And they expected Ed Catmull — Pixar's president — to walk in and use his authority to clean house.

He had the power to fire people.
He had the power to restructure the team.
He had the power to make an example out of someone.
He had the power to show who was in charge.

Instead, he stunned everyone.

He refused to fire anyone.
He refused to shame anyone.
He refused to weaponize his authority.

He said:

"The problem isn't the people.
The problem is the environment we created for them."

Then he did something even more powerful:

He took responsibility.

"If the team is failing, leadership failed first."

That moment changed Pixar's culture forever.

The team rallied.
The film was rebuilt from scratch.
Toy Story 2 became one of the most successful animated sequels in history.

And the people who lived through that moment said the same thing:

"Ed earned our respect because he didn't use his power to punish us.
He used it to protect us."

That's leadership.
That's restraint.
That's Week 42.

Power Is a Tool — Not a Weapon

Weak leaders use power to:

- intimidate
- control
- silence
- elevate themselves
- protect their ego
- avoid accountability

Strong leaders use power to:

- protect their people
- enforce standards fairly
- create clarity
- build trust
- elevate others
- take responsibility

Power in the hands of a weak leader becomes a weapon.
Power in the hands of a strong leader becomes a tool.

The Most Dangerous Moment in Leadership

The most dangerous moment isn't when you're overwhelmed.

It's when you're comfortable.

Because comfort breeds:

- entitlement
- arrogance
- shortcuts
- favoritism
- emotional laziness
- the belief that rules apply to others, not you

Power whispers lies:

"You've earned this."
"You deserve special treatment."
"No one will question you."
"You're above the standard."

Leaders who believe those lies lose themselves — and their people — long before they lose their position.

The Discipline of Handling Power Well

Leaders who handle power responsibly:

- stay humble
- stay consistent
- stay fair
- stay grounded
- stay accountable
- stay connected to their people
- stay aware of how their actions ripple outward

They understand that power isn't something you *own*.
It's something you *borrow*.

And the people you lead decide whether you get to keep it.

The Emotional Maturity Behind "Just Because I Can Doesn't Mean I Should"

One of the most powerful leadership mindsets is:

"Just because I can... doesn't mean I should."

That's restraint.
That's discipline.
That's character.

And people trust leaders who choose restraint over ego.

The Signs You're Growing Into This Truth

You start noticing:

- you don't need to win every argument
- you don't need to be the loudest voice
- you don't need to remind people of your authority
- you treat everyone with dignity, regardless of rank or role
- you give credit freely and take blame willingly
- you enforce standards without favoritism
- you use your influence to lift others, not yourself

This isn't weakness.
This is strength under control.

The Leaders People Follow Willingly

People follow leaders who:

- handle power with humility
- stay steady when others would flex
- use authority to protect, not dominate
- stay grounded when success arrives
- never forget where they came from
- never forget who they serve

Power doesn't corrupt leaders.
It reveals them.

Leadership Takeaway

Leadership isn't measured by how much power you have.
It's measured by how you handle the power you're given.

The moment you realize that power is a responsibility — not a privilege — is the moment you stop using leadership to elevate yourself... and start using it to elevate others.

WEEK 43

THE MOMENT YOU REALIZE YOUR REPUTATION ARRIVES BEFORE YOU DO

"Your reputation walks into the room before you do. Make sure it's working for you, not against you." — *Todd Fritz*

The Moment You Finally Understand

There's a moment in leadership when you realize something that changes how you carry yourself forever:

People form an opinion of you long before you speak.
Your reputation speaks first.

Your reputation is your shadow.
It enters the room ahead of you.
It shapes expectations before you open your mouth.
It influences trust before you give direction.
It determines whether people lean in... or brace.

And here's the part most leaders underestimate:

You don't build your reputation in the big moments.
You build it in the small ones.

The Shadow You Don't Control in the Moment

Leaders often think their reputation is shaped by:

- big speeches
- big decisions
- big accomplishments
- big crises

But the truth is simpler — and harder:

Your reputation is built by the patterns people see in you.

- how you treat people who can't help you
- how you behave when you're tired
- how you respond when you're wrong
- how you talk about people when they're not in the room
- how consistent you are when no one is watching
- how you handle pressure, power, and disappointment

Your reputation is the sum of your habits.

A Real Story — Patagonia's "Don't Buy This Jacket" Moment

In 2011, Patagonia was preparing for Black Friday — the biggest retail day of the year.
Every brand was gearing up to push volume, drive revenue, and dominate the outdoor market.

Patagonia's leadership team met to finalize their campaign.

They had the power to:

- flood the market
- push aggressive sales
- ride the holiday wave
- maximize profit

Instead, CEO **Yvon Chouinard** made a decision that stunned the entire company.

He said:

"We're going to tell customers *not* to buy our product."

People thought he was joking.

He wasn't.

He ordered a full-page New York Times ad with a giant photo of their bestselling jacket and the headline:

"DON'T BUY THIS JACKET."

The ad explained the environmental cost of manufacturing it — water usage, carbon footprint, materials impact — and encouraged customers to:

- repair what they already owned
- buy only what they needed
- think before consuming

This wasn't a marketing stunt.
It was a leadership decision rooted in values.

And here's the part that matters for Week 43:

Patagonia's reputation for integrity walked into the room before the ad ever did.

For years, they had:

- repaired gear for free
- encouraged customers to reuse
- donated profits
- prioritized environmental responsibility
- lived their values quietly

So when they said “Don’t buy this jacket,” people believed them.

Their reputation made the message credible.

And the result?

- Sales increased — not from hype, but from trust
- Customer loyalty skyrocketed
- Patagonia became the gold standard for values-driven leadership
- Their reputation became their competitive advantage

The ad didn’t create their reputation.
It revealed it.

And that’s the leadership truth:

Your reputation arrives before you do — and Patagonia’s reputation made that moment possible.

Reputation Is a Leadership Multiplier — or a Leadership Tax

Your reputation either:

Multiplies your influence

People trust you faster.
They follow you sooner.
They give you the benefit of the doubt.
They bring you problems early.
They believe your intentions.

Or it taxes your influence

People hesitate.
They hold back.
They question your motives.
They wait to see if you're consistent.
They protect themselves instead of trusting you.

Your reputation determines whether leadership is uphill or downhill.

How Reputations Are Built — and Broken

Reputations are built through:

- consistency
- fairness
- humility
- emotional steadiness
- honesty
- follow-through
- how you treat people when you don't need anything from them

Reputations are broken through:

- hypocrisy
- ego
- volatility
- favoritism
- broken promises
- talking one way and acting another
- using people instead of developing them

Reputation is slow to build and fast to lose.

The Discipline of Protecting Your Shadow

Leaders who understand the power of reputation:

- guard their integrity
- stay consistent in public and private
- treat everyone with dignity
- own their mistakes
- keep their word
- stay steady under pressure
- understand that every interaction leaves a mark

They know their reputation is not a performance.
It's a pattern.

The Emotional Maturity Behind "My Actions Are My Brand"

One of the most powerful leadership realizations is:

"My behavior is my brand."

Not your title.
Not your résumé.
Not your accomplishments.

Your behavior.

People don't remember what you *say*.
They remember what you *do*.

The Signs You're Growing Into This Truth

You start noticing:

- you think before reacting
- you treat every interaction as a reflection of your character
- you understand that consistency matters more than charisma

- you stop trying to manage impressions and start managing behavior
- you realize your reputation is built one moment at a time
- you take responsibility for the shadow you cast

This isn't image management.
This is leadership maturity.

The Leaders People Trust Instantly

People trust leaders who:

- are predictable in the best way
- are steady under pressure
- are honest even when it's hard
- are fair even when it's inconvenient
- are humble even when they succeed
- are the same person in every room

Your reputation is your leadership résumé — and people read it long before they read your words.

Leadership Takeaway

Your reputation walks into the room before you do.
Make sure it's working for you, not against you.

Because leadership isn't just what you do today.
It's what people remember about you tomorrow.

WEEK 44

THE MOMENT YOU REALIZE BEING RIGHT ISN'T THE GOAL — BEING RESPONSIBLE IS

"Leadership isn't about proving you're right. It's about taking responsibility when it matters." — Todd Fritz

The Moment You Finally Understand

There's a point in every leader's journey when the ego finally quiets down and a deeper truth settles in:

Being right doesn't move people.
Being responsible does.

You can win arguments and still lose trust.
You can be technically correct and still emotionally wrong.
You can have the best idea in the room and still fail as a leader if you weaponize it.

Mature leaders learn that leadership isn't about scoring points.
It's about carrying weight.

The Trap of Needing to Be Right

Leaders who are addicted to being right:

- interrupt
- correct unnecessarily
- defend their ideas at all costs
- turn discussions into competitions
- make people feel small
- confuse intelligence with leadership

And here's the truth they eventually learn:

People don't follow leaders who need to win.
They follow leaders who take responsibility.

A Real Story — Microsoft's Surface RT Failure and the Leadership Moment That Followed

In 2012, Microsoft launched the Surface RT tablet.
It was supposed to be their answer to the iPad.
The pressure was enormous.
The expectations were sky-high.

But the product wasn't ready.

The operating system confused customers.
The app ecosystem was thin.
Retailers struggled to explain what it could and couldn't do.
Reviews were harsh.

The launch failed — publicly and expensively.

Microsoft was forced to take a **$900 million write-down** on unsold inventory.
That number alone could have triggered a corporate blame-fest.

But here's the leadership moment that mattered.

Steve Ballmer — the CEO at the time — didn't blame engineering.
He didn't blame marketing.
He didn't blame the product team.
He didn't blame the market.

He said, internally and publicly:

"This one's on me.
We built a product people didn't want."

He owned the decision to push the product to market.
He owned the misread of customer needs.
He owned the failure.

And inside Microsoft, something shifted.

Engineers later said:

"That was the moment he became our leader.
Not when he was right — but when he owned being wrong."

That's the truth of Week 44.
Being right is ego.
Being responsible is leadership.

Responsibility Is the Currency of Leadership

Being right is about ego.
Being responsible is about service.

Leaders who choose responsibility:

- protect their people
- absorb pressure
- own mistakes
- share credit
- correct course without shame
- model humility
- create psychological safety

Responsibility builds credibility.
Credibility builds trust.
Trust builds influence.

The Discipline of Letting Go of "Winning"

Leaders who mature past the need to be right:

- ask more questions
- listen without preparing a rebuttal
- stay curious instead of defensive
- prioritize clarity over victory
- focus on outcomes, not arguments
- treat mistakes as data, not threats

They understand that leadership isn't a debate.
It's stewardship.

The Emotional Maturity Behind "This One's on Me"

One of the most powerful sentences a leader can say is:

"This one's on me."

Not as a performance.
Not as a tactic.
But as truth.

Responsibility is magnetic.
It pulls people toward you.
It makes them want to follow you.
It makes them want to give their best.

Because people don't need perfect leaders.
They need accountable ones.

The Signs You're Growing Into This Truth

You start noticing:

- you don't need to win every disagreement
- you care more about outcomes than credit
- you admit mistakes faster
- you listen longer
- you ask for input earlier
- you stop defending your ego and start defending your people
- you understand that responsibility is leadership's foundation

This isn't weakness.
This is strength without insecurity.

The Leaders People Trust Instinctively

People trust leaders who:

- own their decisions
- own their mistakes
- own their impact
- own their influence
- own the culture they create
- own the weight of leadership

Responsibility is the quiet force that separates leaders from performers.

Leadership Takeaway

Being right is about you.
Being responsible is about everyone you lead.

The moment you stop trying to win and start trying to serve is the moment you become the leader people remember.

WEEK 45

THE MOMENT YOU REALIZE LEADERSHIP IS WHAT HAPPENS WHEN YOU'RE NOT IN THE ROOM

"Your real leadership shows up in the conversations you'll never hear." — *Todd Fritz*

The Moment You Finally Understand

There's a moment in leadership when you realize something that changes everything:

Your influence isn't measured by what happens when you're present.
It's measured by what happens when you're absent.

Anyone can look like a leader when they're standing in front of the room.
Anyone can sound like a leader when they're giving direction.
Anyone can act like a leader when people are watching.

But the real test is simple:

What do people do when you're not there?

That's your leadership.
That's your culture.
That's your legacy.

The Illusion of Presence

Many leaders confuse presence with influence.

They think:

- "If I'm in the room, things will go right."
- "If I'm watching, people will perform."
- "If I'm involved, the standard will hold."

But that's not leadership.
That's supervision.

Leadership is when the standard holds without you.
Leadership is when people do the right thing because it's who they are — not because you're standing there.

A Real Story — The RitzCarlton Card Nobody Asked For

RitzCarlton is famous for customer service, but here's the part most people don't know:

Every employee — from housekeeping to the front desk to maintenance — has the authority to spend up to **$2,000 per guest** to solve a problem.

No manager approval.
No forms.
No escalation.
No waiting.

Why?

Because the company understands a simple truth:

Leadership is what happens when the leader isn't there.

One story stands out.

A family checked out of a RitzCarlton hotel and realized, after arriving home, that their child's stuffed giraffe — "Joshie" — had been left behind.

The father called the hotel, embarrassed, hoping it had been found.

The housekeeping team located the toy.
They could have simply mailed it back.

Instead, without being told, without a policy, without a manager directing them, the team created an entire experience:

- They took photos of Joshie lounging by the pool
- They made him a guest badge
- They documented his "extended vacation"
- They packaged everything with a handwritten note

They didn't do this because someone was watching.
They didn't do this because a leader was in the room.
They didn't do this because they were told to.

They did it because the culture had been built so well that the standard lived inside them.

That's leadership.

Not presence.
Not supervision.
Not control.

Culture.

The Quiet Power of Culture You've Built

When you're not in the room, people reveal:

- whether they trust each other
- whether they cut corners
- whether they speak honestly
- whether they protect the standard
- whether they take ownership
- whether they treat others with dignity
- whether they act with integrity

If they do these things without you, you're leading.
If they only do them when you're present, you're managing.

The Discipline of Leading Through Influence, Not Proximity

Leaders who understand this truth:

- build systems, not dependencies
- build trust, not fear
- build clarity, not confusion
- build ownership, not compliance
- build people who can operate without them

They don't need to hover.
They don't need to micromanage.
They don't need to be everywhere.

Because they've built something that stands on its own.

The Emotional Maturity Behind "They Don't Need Me There"

One of the most liberating leadership realizations is:

"If I've done my job well, they don't need me in the room."

Not because you're irrelevant.
But because you've built capability.
You've built confidence.
You've built clarity.
You've built trust.

And that's the point.

Leadership isn't about being indispensable.
It's about being impactful.

The Signs You're Growing Into This Truth

You start noticing:

- meetings run well without you
- people make decisions aligned with your values
- standards hold without reminders
- problems get solved before they reach you
- people speak honestly even when you're not present
- the culture feels stable, not dependent
- your absence doesn't create anxiety

This is the moment you realize you're not just leading tasks.
You're leading people.

The Leaders People Remember

People remember leaders who:

- build trust
- build clarity
- build capability
- build confidence
- build a culture that outlives them

Your leadership isn't measured by how things go when you're in the room.
It's measured by how things go when you're not.

Leadership Takeaway

Your real leadership shows up in the conversations you'll never hear.

Because the true measure of a leader isn't presence.
It's the culture they leave behind.

WEEK 46

THE MOMENT YOU REALIZE YOUR JOB IS TO DEVELOP LEADERS, NOT FOLLOWERS

"Don't build followers. Build successors." — *Todd Fritz*

The Moment You Finally Understand

There's a moment in leadership when you stop measuring your success by what *you* can do and start measuring it by what **others** can do because of you.

That's when it hits you:

Leadership isn't about creating dependence.
It's about creating capability.

Followers need direction.
Leaders need development.

And your legacy isn't built by how well you perform.
It's built by how well your people perform when you're not there.

The Trap of Being the Only One Who Can Do It

Early in a leader's career, being the goto person feels good.

You know the answers.
You solve the problems.
You carry the load.
You become indispensable.

But here's the truth:

If everything depends on you, you're not leading—you're bottlenecking.

Real leaders don't hoard competence.
They multiply it.

A Real Story — Howard Schultz and the Starbucks Leadership Rebuild

When Howard Schultz returned to Starbucks in 2008, the company was slipping.

Quality had dropped.
Culture was fading.
Customer trust was eroding.
Leaders were overwhelmed and underdeveloped.

Schultz didn't come back to be the hero.
He came back to build leaders who could run the company without him.

And he made a decision almost no CEO of a global brand would make:

He shut down every Starbucks in America for a three-hour training session.

All 7,100 stores.
All at once.
Millions in lost revenue.

Why?

Because Schultz believed something you believe:

If your people aren't trained, you're not leading — you're hoping.

But here's the part that fits Week 46 perfectly:

Schultz didn't lead the training.
He trained the leaders to lead the training.

He told his store managers:

"You are the stewards of this company.
You are the ones who will rebuild it.
Not me."

He didn't want 7,100 stores dependent on him.
He wanted 7,100 leaders capable of carrying the mission without him.

And it worked.

Quality improved.
Culture stabilized.
Customer trust returned.
The leadership bench strengthened.

A regional director later said:

"Howard didn't rebuild Starbucks.
He rebuilt the leaders who rebuilt Starbucks."

That's the heart of Week 46.
Not hero leadership.
Not savior leadership.
Multiplying leadership.

The Shift From Doing to Developing

Leaders who understand this truth stop asking:

"How do I get this done?"

And start asking:

"Who can I develop to do this next time?"

They shift from:

solving problems
to
teaching people how to solve problems

giving answers
to
asking questions that build judgment

being the hero
to
building heroes

This is the moment leadership becomes scalable.

The Discipline of Letting Others Step Up

Developing leaders requires discipline:

letting others take the lead
letting them struggle
letting them own decisions
letting them learn through experience
letting go of perfection
letting go of control

It's slower at first.
It's messier at first.
It's uncomfortable at first.

But it's the only path to real leadership impact.

The Emotional Maturity Behind "Replace Me"

Most leaders never say it.
Even fewer mean it.

But the ones who do — the ones who genuinely want their people to surpass them — those are the leaders who leave a mark.

"Replace me" isn't insecurity.
It's confidence.
It's humility.
It's legacy.

It means:

"I'm not building followers.
I'm building the next generation."

The Signs You're Growing Into This Truth

You start noticing:

you delegate development, not just tasks
you give people room to think, not just room to work
you stop being the smartest person in the room on purpose
you celebrate when someone outperforms you
you invest in potential, not just performance
you build systems that outlast you
you want your people to win even when you're not there to see it

This is the moment leadership becomes generational.

The Leaders People Never Forget

People never forget leaders who:

saw potential in them
invested in them
challenged them

trusted them
prepared them
promoted them
believed in them before they believed in themselves

Your legacy isn't what you did.
It's who you built.

Leadership Takeaway

If you're the only one who can do it, you're not leading—you're limiting.

Train them to replace you.
That's how you build leaders.
That's how you build culture.
That's how you build legacy.

WEEK 47

THE MOMENT YOU REALIZE TRUST IS BUILT BY CONSISTENCY

*"Anyone can be impressive for a moment.
Leaders are consistent for a lifetime." — Todd Fritz*

The Moment You Finally Understand

There's a moment in leadership when you stop being impressed by intensity.

Intensity is loud.
Intensity is emotional.
Intensity is dramatic.
Intensity looks like leadership — for a moment.

But then you learn the truth:

Intensity inspires people.
Consistency transforms them.

Anyone can show up big once.
Anyone can deliver a great speech.

Anyone can have a burst of motivation.
Anyone can be excellent on their best day.

But leadership isn't measured on your best day.
It's measured on your *everyday*.

The Illusion of Intensity

Intensity feels powerful because it's visible.

People notice:

- the passionate speech
- the late-night push
- the heroic save
- the big moment
- the dramatic turnaround

But intensity is a spike.
It rises fast and fades faster.

Consistency is the opposite.
It's quiet.
It's steady.
It's predictable.
It's reliable.
It's boring to the untrained eye.

But consistency is what builds trust.
Consistency is what builds culture.
Consistency is what builds leaders.

A Real Story — Tim Duncan and the Spurs' Dynasty of Consistency

In an era defined by highlight reels, trash talk, and emotional fireworks, Tim Duncan led the San Antonio Spurs with something far more powerful:

Consistency.

No theatrics.
No ego.
No emotional roller-coasters.
No "look at me" leadership.

Just the same steady presence every single day.

Win or lose, Duncan's tone never changed.
After championships, he was calm.
After tough losses, he was calm.
After great games or bad ones — calm.

Gregg Popovich, one of the greatest coaches in NBA history, said:

"Timmy allowed us to be consistent because he was consistent."

His teammates trusted him because he was predictable in the best way:

- he showed up
- he worked
- he stayed humble
- he held the standard
- he never made it about himself

And the result?

A 19year run of excellence:

- 5 NBA championships
- 19 straight winning seasons

- 19 straight playoff appearances
- the highest winning percentage of any player in NBA history

A teammate once said:

**"Tim didn't lead with speeches.
He led with the same standard every day."**

That's leadership.
Not fireworks.
Foundation.

Why Consistency Wins

Consistency creates:

- trust
- stability
- clarity
- predictability
- confidence
- alignment
- culture

Intensity creates moments.
Consistency creates momentum.

Intensity gets attention.
Consistency earns respect.

Intensity motivates people.
Consistency develops them.

Intensity is emotional.
Consistency is professional.

The Discipline of Showing Up the Same Way Every Day

Consistency requires discipline:

- steady tone
- steady expectations
- steady standards
- steady accountability
- steady presence
- steady emotional regulation

It's not glamorous.
It's not dramatic.
It's not Instagram-worthy.

But it's what separates leaders from performers.

The Emotional Maturity Behind "I Don't Need to Be Impressive"

There's a moment when you stop trying to impress people and start trying to **support** them.

You realize:

- they don't need your intensity
- they need your steadiness
- they don't need your speeches
- they need your reliability
- they don't need your fire
- they need your foundation

Consistency is emotional maturity in motion.

The Signs You're Growing Into This Truth

You start noticing:

- you don't chase big moments
- you value routines more than adrenaline
- you stay steady when others spike
- you enforce standards without theatrics
- you show up the same on good days and bad
- you understand that trust is built in repetition
- you realize leadership is a pattern, not a performance

This is the moment leadership becomes sustainable.

The Leaders People Trust With Their Future

People trust leaders who:

- are predictable in the best way
- don't change with the weather
- don't let emotions dictate standards
- don't need to be the hero
- don't burn hot and disappear
- don't spike under pressure
- don't surprise their team with volatility

Consistency is the quiet superpower of leadership.

Leadership Takeaway

Intensity is impressive.
Consistency is transformative.

Anyone can show up big once.
Leaders show up steady every day.

WEEK 48

THE MOMENT YOU REALIZE PEOPLE DON'T NEED CERTAINTY — THEY NEED CLARITY

*"People don't need you to predict the future.
They need you to light the path." — Todd Fritz*

The Moment You Finally Understand

There's a moment in leadership when you realize something that changes everything:

People don't need you to have all the answers.
They don't need you to predict the future.
They don't need you to remove uncertainty.

They need you to **bring clarity into uncertainty**.

Clarity is direction.
Clarity is alignment.
Clarity is confidence.
Clarity is leadership.

The Myth of Certainty

Many leaders burn themselves out trying to create certainty.

They think:

- "I need to know everything before I speak."
- "I need the perfect plan."
- "I need to eliminate all risk."
- "I need to guarantee the outcome."

But certainty is a myth.
The world changes too fast.
Information is incomplete.
Variables shift.
People move.
Markets move.
Life moves.

If you wait for certainty, you'll never lead.

What People Actually Need

People don't need certainty.
They need:

- clarity of purpose
- clarity of priorities
- clarity of expectations
- clarity of roles
- clarity of the next step
- clarity of what matters most

Clarity reduces fear.
Clarity creates alignment.
Clarity builds trust.

Certainty is impossible.
Clarity is a choice.

A Real Story — Captain "Sully" Sullenberger and the Hudson River Landing

When US Airways Flight 1549 lost both engines over New York City, Captain Chesley "Sully" Sullenberger had **208 seconds** to make a decision.

No time for certainty.
No time for analysis.
No time for perfect information.

He had:

- incomplete data
- conflicting warnings
- a crippled aircraft
- terrified passengers
- a city below him

But he had clarity.

He told air traffic control:

"We're gonna be in the Hudson."

Not "maybe."
Not "we'll see."
Not "we're evaluating options."

Clarity.

That clarity aligned the crew.
It aligned the cabin.
It aligned the response.
It saved 155 lives.

After the landing, investigators asked him how he made the decision so quickly.

He said:

"In uncertainty, you don't need more information.
You need clarity about what matters."

That's leadership.

Not certainty.
Clarity.

Why Clarity Wins

Clarity:

- calms people
- focuses effort
- reduces confusion
- accelerates decisions
- builds confidence
- creates unity
- eliminates noise

People can move without certainty.
They cannot move without clarity.

The Discipline of Clear Leadership

Clear leaders:

- speak simply
- define priorities
- eliminate ambiguity
- repeat what matters
- align people to purpose
- communicate early
- communicate often
- communicate plainly

They don't hide behind jargon.
They don't over-complicate.
They don't confuse motion with progress.

They make things understandable.

The Emotional Maturity Behind "Here's What We're Doing"

There's a moment when you stop trying to impress people with complexity and start serving them with clarity.

You realize:

- clarity is kindness
- clarity is respect
- clarity is leadership

People don't follow the smartest leader.
They follow the clearest one.

The Signs You're Growing Into This Truth

You start noticing:

- you communicate earlier, not later
- you simplify instead of complicate
- you repeat the mission without apology
- you define the next step, not the whole journey
- you stop trying to sound impressive
- you start trying to be understood
- you lead people through uncertainty instead of trying to eliminate it

This is the moment leadership becomes communication, not performance.

The Leaders People Trust in Uncertain Times

People trust leaders who:

- speak plainly
- reduce confusion
- define direction
- stay steady
- stay simple
- stay clear

Clarity is the anchor in chaos.

Leadership Takeaway

You'll never eliminate uncertainty.
But you can eliminate confusion.

People don't need certainty.
They need clarity.

WEEK 49

THE MOMENT YOU REALIZE YOU ARE THE EMOTIONAL CEILING

"Your team rises to your steadiness or sinks to your volatility."
— Todd Fritz

The Moment You Finally Understand

There's a moment in leadership when you realize something uncomfortable but liberating:

Your team will never be more emotionally stable than you are.

Your calm becomes their calm.
Your panic becomes their panic.
Your steadiness becomes their stability.
Your volatility becomes their chaos.

You set the emotional ceiling.
You set the emotional floor.
You set the emotional tone.

Not with speeches.
Not with policies.
Not with mission statements.

With your **regulation**.

The Myth of "I'm Just Being Honest"

Some leaders justify emotional outbursts as authenticity.

"I'm just being real."
"I'm just passionate."
"I'm just frustrated."
"I'm just telling it like it is."

But here's the truth:

**Your people don't experience your emotions as honesty.
They experience them as instability.**

Your reaction becomes their reality.

The Weight of Being the Emotional Ceiling

Being the emotional ceiling means:

- you stay steady when others spike
- you stay calm when others panic
- you stay grounded when others drift
- you stay measured when others escalate
- you stay rational when others get emotional

This isn't suppression.
It's leadership.

A Real Story — Admiral William McRaven and the Bin Laden Raid

During the 2011 raid on Osama bin Laden's compound, Admiral William McRaven served as the overall mission commander. He wasn't on the ground — he was in the operations center, overseeing every second of one of the most dangerous and consequential missions in modern history.

And here's what everyone in that room said afterward:

McRaven never changed his tone.
Not once.

During the raid:

- a helicopter crashed inside the compound
- communications were unstable
- timelines shifted
- unknown threats emerged
- the world was watching without knowing it

And McRaven stayed calm.

No raised voice.
No panic.
No emotional spike.
No visible stress.

Just steady, measured, controlled leadership.

A CIA analyst later said:

"When the helicopter went down, everyone looked at McRaven.
He didn't flinch.
So no one else did either."

His emotional regulation became the emotional ceiling for:

- the operators on the ground

- the pilots
- the intelligence teams
- the White House Situation Room
- the entire mission

Afterward, McRaven explained his approach:

**"If I lose my composure, I lose the room.
If I lose the room, I lose the mission."**

That's the emotional ceiling in its purest form.

He didn't match the chaos.
He anchored it.

He didn't react.
He regulated.

He didn't spike.
He steadied the entire operation.

Why Emotional Regulation Wins

Your emotional steadiness:

- lowers fear
- increases trust
- improves decision-making
- reduces mistakes
- stabilizes culture
- protects psychological safety
- creates confidence under pressure

People don't need a leader who feels what they feel.
They need a leader who can **hold** what they feel.

The Discipline of Emotional Leadership

Being the emotional ceiling requires discipline:

- controlling tone
- controlling pace
- controlling volume
- controlling reactions
- controlling assumptions
- controlling your internal temperature

Not because you're suppressing emotion.
Because you're **stewarding** it.

The Emotional Maturity Behind "I Go First"

There's a moment when you realize:

- you go first in calm
- you go first in clarity
- you go first in steadiness
- you go first in composure
- you go first in emotional discipline

Your team mirrors you.
Not your words — **you**.

The Signs You're Growing Into This Truth

You start noticing:

- you pause before reacting
- you lower your voice when others raise theirs
- you ask questions instead of making assumptions
- you stay steady when others get emotional
- you regulate yourself before you regulate the room
- you understand that your presence is the thermostat

This is the moment leadership becomes emotional intelligence, not emotional expression.

The Leaders People Trust in Crisis

People trust leaders who:

- stay calm
- stay clear
- stay steady
- stay rational
- stay grounded
- stay composed

Your emotional ceiling becomes their emotional safety.

Leadership Takeaway

Your team doesn't rise to your expectations.
They rise to your **regulation**.

You are the emotional ceiling.
Lead like it.

WEEK 50

THE MOMENT YOU REALIZE LEADERSHIP IS STEWARDSHIP, NOT OWNERSHIP

"You don't own the role. You're entrusted with it." — Todd Fritz

The Moment You Finally Understand

There's a moment in leadership when something shifts deep inside you.

You stop seeing your position as something you *earned*
and start seeing it as something you're *responsible for.*

You stop thinking in terms of **my team**, **my people**, **my program**, **my mission**
and start thinking in terms of:

"I'm the caretaker of something bigger than me."

That's stewardship.
And it's one of the highest forms of leadership.

**Ownership Is About Control.

Stewardship Is About Responsibility.**

Ownership says:

- "This is mine."
- "I decide."
- "I control the outcome."

Stewardship says:

- "This was entrusted to me."
- "I'm responsible for its health."
- "I must leave it better than I found it."

Ownership is ego.
Stewardship is maturity.

The Weight of Stewardship

When you embrace stewardship, you realize:

- you're responsible for the culture
- you're responsible for the standard
- you're responsible for the people
- you're responsible for the future
- you're responsible for the hand-off

You're not the owner.
You're the guardian.

You're not the hero.
You're the caretaker.

You're not the center.
You're the steward.

A Real Story — Theodore Roosevelt and the Stewardship of America's National Parks

When Theodore Roosevelt became President, he didn't see America's wilderness as something he *owned*.
He saw it as something he was **responsible for**.

He believed the natural beauty of the United States didn't belong to him, or even to the people alive at the time.

He believed it belonged to:

- future generations
- children not yet born
- Americans he would never meet

So he acted like a steward, not an owner.

During his presidency, Roosevelt:

- created 5 national parks
- established 18 national monuments
- protected 150 national forests
- preserved over 230 million acres of land

He wasn't thinking in election cycles.
He was thinking in **generational cycles**.

He fought political pressure, industrial interests, and short-term thinking because he believed:

"The nation behaves well if it treats the natural resources as assets which it must turn over to the next generation increased, and not impaired."

A historian later said:

**"Roosevelt didn't preserve land.
He preserved the future."**

That's stewardship in its purest form.

He didn't protect the land for himself.
He protected it for the next century.

He didn't build something for his legacy.
He built something that didn't need his name at all.

Why Stewardship Wins

Stewardship creates:

- continuity
- stability
- legacy
- trust
- humility
- longevity
- resilience

Ownership creates dependency.
Stewardship creates durability.

Ownership ends when you leave.
Stewardship continues long after you're gone.

The Discipline of Being a Steward

Stewards:

- protect the standard
- develop successors
- honor the past
- strengthen the present
- prepare the future
- make decisions that outlast them
- think generationally, not personally

They don't ask, "What do I want?"
They ask, "What does this need?"

The Emotional Maturity Behind "This Isn't About Me"

There's a moment when you stop trying to build a legacy with your name on it
and start trying to build a legacy that doesn't need your name at all.

You realize:

- the mission matters more than your ego
- the people matter more than your preferences
- the future matters more than your comfort

That's stewardship.
That's leadership at altitude.

The Signs You're Growing Into This Truth

You start noticing:

- you think longterm, not short-term
- you develop people who can replace you
- you protect the culture instead of your pride
- you make decisions that outlive your tenure
- you stop chasing credit
- you start chasing continuity
- you care more about the hand-off than the spotlight

This is the moment leadership becomes legacy.

The Leaders People Trust With the Future

People trust leaders who:

- think beyond themselves
- build systems that last
- develop leaders who lead
- protect what matters
- leave things better than they found them

Stewardship is the highest form of leadership.

Leadership Takeaway

You don't own the role.
You're entrusted with it.

Leave it better than you found it.

WEEK 51

THE MOMENT YOU REALIZE LEADERSHIP IS BUILT IN THE QUIET DECISIONS NO ONE SEES

"Your legacy is shaped by the choices you make when no one is watching." — *Todd Fritz*

The Moment You Finally Understand

There comes a point in leadership — late, usually — when you realize something uncomfortable:

The loud moments don't define you.
The quiet ones do.

Not the speeches.
Not the ceremonies.
Not the big wins.
Not the public praise.

It's the decisions you make alone.
The choices no one knows about.
The discipline no one applauds.
The integrity no one witnesses.

That's where leadership is actually forged.

The Public Moments Are Just the Echo

People think leadership is built in:

- the big meetings
- the big calls
- the big crises
- the big announcements

But those moments are just the **echo** of the work you did in private.

The real leadership happens when:

- you choose honesty over convenience
- you choose fairness over favoritism
- you choose discipline over comfort
- you choose what's right over what's easy
- you choose responsibility over ego

No spotlight.
No audience.
No applause.

Just you and your character.

A Real Story — Abraham Lincoln and the Unseen Pardons

During the Civil War, Abraham Lincoln carried the weight of a nation tearing itself apart.

But late at night, after the meetings, after the generals, after the chaos, Lincoln would sit alone in his dimly lit office with a stack of military court-martial cases.

Young Union soldiers — boys, really — sentenced to death for desertion or falling asleep on guard duty.

No cameras.
No advisors.
No political gain.

Just a tired man reading the stories of scared, exhausted kids.

And more often than not, he wrote one word:

"Pardoned."

He believed:

- fear makes boys run
- exhaustion makes boys sleep
- mercy makes men loyal

He didn't announce these decisions.
He didn't publicize them.
He didn't use them to shape his image.

He made them because they were right.

A Union general later said:

"The nation will never know how many sons Lincoln quietly gave back to their mothers."

That's leadership in its purest form.

Quiet.
Unseen.
Uncelebrated.
But deeply, profoundly human.

Why Quiet Decisions Matter

Quiet decisions:

- shape culture
- build trust
- reveal character
- protect standards
- define integrity
- create loyalty
- determine legacy

People may never know what you did.
But they will always feel who you are.

The Discipline of Unseen Leadership

Quiet leadership requires:

- restraint
- humility
- patience
- emotional maturity
- moral clarity
- consistency
- courage

It's easy to perform in public.
It's hard to be principled in private.

That's why quiet decisions matter more.

The Moment You Realize the Truth

You eventually understand:

- your reputation is public
- your character is private
- your influence is public
- your integrity is private
- your leadership is public
- your legacy is private

And the private always outweighs the public.

Always.

The Signs You're Growing Into This Truth

You start noticing:

- you make decisions based on values, not optics
- you choose longterm trust over short-term approval
- you correct yourself before anyone else needs to
- you hold standards even when no one is watching
- you do the right thing even when it costs you
- you stop performing and start becoming

This is the moment leadership becomes internal, not external.

The Leaders People Trust the Most

People trust leaders who:

- do the right thing quietly
- make decisions without needing credit
- protect others without announcing it
- choose integrity without witnesses
- carry weight without applause

Quiet leadership is the highest form of leadership.

Leadership Takeaway

Your loudest moments won't define you.
Your quietest ones will.

Lead well when no one is watching.

WEEK 52

THE DAY MY HEART STOPPED LEADING

"If you can breathe, you have opportunity. Take that opportunity."
— Todd Fritz

People imagine heart attacks as dramatic events — clutching the chest, collapsing in slow motion, a clear warning that something is wrong.

Mine didn't give me that courtesy.

It was a quiet day at home. My partner was upstairs in the washroom. I was downstairs alone. Nothing unusual. Nothing alarming. Just a moment of what felt like acid reflux — a little burn in the chest, a few seconds of sweating.

And then the world changed.

There was no ramp-up.
No tingling.
No cinematic warning.

Just an instant, catastrophic collapse.

A crushing force slammed into my chest so violently it drove me to my knees. It felt like the Empire State Building had been dropped onto me, and I was the only thing holding it up. My body folded into the fetal position. I vomited and defecated uncontrollably as my extremities curled inward — the unmistakable sign that parts of me were already dying.

I didn't know what was happening.

But I knew one thing with absolute clarity:

I was dying.

And that made me angry.

Not scared.
Not panicked.
Angry.

Because I wasn't done.
Because this wasn't how my story was supposed to end.
Because I had more to do, more to give, more to lead.

Even as the pain tore through me, I remember thinking:

No. Not like this. Not today.

I don't remember much after that.

When I woke up in the hospital, I wasn't emotional. I wasn't reflective. I wasn't grateful. I was in diagnostic mode — the same mode that's kept me alive in war zones and dangerous jobs my whole life.

What's wrong.
How do I fix it.
Get me out of this bed.

The doctors told me I had suffered a widow-maker — a 100% blockage of the LAD. Nearly an hour without blood flow. Most people don't survive that. Many never make it to the hospital. Some die before they hit the floor.

But I was still breathing.

And if you can breathe, you have opportunity.

I begged the staff to let me walk. They refused at first — my ejection fraction was so low they didn't trust my heart to handle anything. But I kept pushing. Eventually they relented, and I walked laps around the cardiac floor for hours every day, dragging my IV lines behind me like a stubborn mule.

And here's the part most people don't know:

I was still in the service.

And the moment the paperwork started moving, the machine tried to spit me out.

Medical boards.
Evaluations.
Doubt.
People deciding my future based on numbers on a chart.

They didn't understand something fundamental about me:

I was still stronger than most of the people trying to retire me.

Six months after my heart attack — six months after dying on my own floor — I deployed to Puerto Rico and the Virgin Islands to perform rescue and relief operations two days after Hurricane Maria hit.

I wasn't supposed to be there.

But I was.

Because I wasn't done.

Recovery wasn't heroic.
It wasn't cinematic.
It was lonely.

I lived alone. My partner was back in Canada. There were nights when the lights upstairs were left on, but I was too weak to climb the stairs to turn them off. I couldn't sleep in my own bed. I couldn't carry groceries. I couldn't walk a flight of stairs without stopping halfway, gasping for air like an old man.

That was the lowest point — not the heart attack itself, but the quiet humiliation of being alive and unable to live.

But every morning, I woke up and told myself the same thing I told myself on the floor that day:

You're still breathing.
If you can breathe, you can fight.
Never quit.

The military beat that into me from day one.

And it saved my life long after I hung up the uniform.

So I fought.
Every day.
Every hour.
Every step.

And when I decided I was going to rebuild myself, I didn't do it halfway.

I trained like a man possessed.
I rebuilt my body from the inside out.
Strict diet.
Relentless exercise.
Hours of meditation.
Discipline that bordered on obsession.

Not to impress anyone — but to reclaim myself.

Nine months after my heart tried to kill me, I placed Top 10 in the Men's Health Ultimate Guy Search.

Not because I wanted a trophy.
Not because I needed validation.
But because I needed to prove something to myself:

I wasn't done.

I'm still not done.

Leadership Takeaway: Leading Yourself Back From the Edge

Leadership isn't always about guiding others.
Sometimes it's about dragging yourself back from the brink when no one is watching.

A widow-maker doesn't just test your heart — it tests your identity.

It forces you to confront the question every leader eventually faces:

Who are you when everything is stripped away?

When you can't climb the stairs.
When you can't sleep in your own bed.
When your body betrays you.
When your future is uncertain.
When no one is there to cheer you on.

Leadership in those moments is simple, brutal, and honest:

If you can breathe, you can fight.
If you can fight, you can rise.
Never quit.

Closing Reflection

I don't think about the widow-maker every day anymore.

But it's always there — a quiet shadow in the corner of the room, a reminder that life doesn't come with guarantees or warnings. It didn't break me, but it stripped me down to the studs and forced me to rebuild with intention.

I keep a grateful-timer app on my phone.
It counts the days, hours, minutes, and seconds I've been given since the attack.

Not as a morbid reminder — but as a compass.

There's a Japanese proverb that says, "Happiness blooms in the garden of gratefulness."

I didn't understand that before.
Now I do.

I used to think strength was measured in how much weight you could carry, how far you could run, how long you could endure.

But strength is quieter than that.

Strength is choosing to stand up when no one would blame you for staying down.
Strength is deciding that breath is enough reason to keep moving.

People see the Men's Health Top 10 finish, the comeback, the deployments, the medals, the titles — but they don't see the nights I couldn't climb the stairs, the mornings I woke up unsure if my heart would hold, the moments I had to convince myself that living was still worth the effort.

But that's the truth of it.
That's the part that matters.

A widow-maker didn't end my life.
It clarified it.

It reminded me that leadership isn't about rank or position — it's about responsibility.
It reminded me that resilience isn't loud — it's stubborn.
It reminded me that purpose isn't found — it's chosen.

And every day since, I've chosen to live with intention.
To lead with humility.
To fight with gratitude.
To breathe with purpose.

Because I'm still here.

And as long as I'm still breathing, I'm not done.

SEASON IV REFLECTION — LEADING

Season IV is where everything becomes real.

This is the season of mortality, legacy, and meaning — the season where leadership stops being theoretical and becomes personal.

You faced the moment every leader eventually meets:
the moment life strips everything away and asks,
"Who are you now?"

Your heart attack wasn't just a medical event.
It was a reckoning.
A mirror.
A reset.
A reminder that leadership isn't about rank or position — it's about responsibility, resilience, and the stubborn decision to rise when no one would blame you for staying down.

Season IV is the season where you learned the most important truth of all:

If you can breathe, you can fight.
If you can fight, you can rise.
Never quit.

This season didn't just close the book.
It clarified it.
It clarified *you*.

FINAL AUTHOR'S NOTE

There's a moment in every leader's life when you realize you've been shaped by more than the titles you held, the missions you completed, or the people you led. You've been shaped by the moments that tested you, humbled you, broke you open, and rebuilt you.

This book wasn't written to impress anyone.
It wasn't written to teach from a pedestal.
It wasn't written to pretend I have all the answers.

It was written because leadership is human.
It's messy.
It's quiet.
It's earned.
And it's lived one moment at a time.

Every week in this book came from a place of truth — moments that shaped me, challenged me, or clarified something I didn't understand until life forced me to. Some were painful. Some were humbling. Some were simple. All of them were real.

If these pages gave you clarity, strength, or a sense of companionship on your own path, then the book did its job.

And if you're still breathing, you're not done.

Keep going.
Keep leading.
Keep becoming.

— Todd Fritz

ACKNOWLEDGMENTS

To the people who shaped me — thank you.

To my partner, whose strength carried me through the darkest seasons of my life. Your presence is the quiet anchor behind every page of this book.

To my daughter, who reminds me every day that leadership begins at home.

To the men and women I served beside — you taught me more about courage, humility, and resilience than any course or classroom ever could.

To the mentors who challenged me, corrected me, and believed in me long before I believed in myself — your fingerprints are on every lesson in this book.

To the medical teams who kept me alive when my heart stopped leading — you gave me the chance to write this.

To the readers who pick up this book — thank you for letting my moments become part of your journey.

And finally, to anyone who has ever stood back up when life tried to keep them down — this book is proof that breath is enough reason to keep fighting.

www.ingramcontent.com/pod-product-compliance
Ingram Content Group UK Ltd.
Pitfield, Milton Keynes, MK11 3LW, UK
UKHW062308290726
14090UKWH00018B/957

9 798995 309802